Nkeiruka

"*Nkeiruka* offers a critical historiographical intervention in Nigerian Adventist studies, blending archival research, ethnographic insight, and historical analysis. Dr. Chigemezi Wogu's forward-looking framework—rooted in eschatological optimism and the Igbo concept of hope—challenges institutional memory and re-centers indigenous agency in mission history. This book is a significant and original contribution to African Christian studies and the global discourse on decolonizing church history."

—CHRISTIE CHUI-SHAN CHOW, author of *Schism: Seventh-day Adventism in Post-Denominational China*

"Chigemezi Wogu is an emerging historian of religion that is worthy of note. His book, *Nkeiruka* fills a void in the genre of Seventh-day Adventist (SDA) historiography on the continent of Africa and indeed the world. His attempt in the book focuses on SDA mission and its history in Nigeria, the most populous black nation in the world. His bottom-up approach is unique, weaving a tapestry of foreign and local cooperation in the progress of Adventism in this country. Local initiatives are explored and highlighted giving a platform for the work of unsung heroes who helped move the work forward. This is done within the context of colonial governmental policies and the emerging independent Nigerian nation. *Nkeruika*, though not the final word on this topic, becomes an important piece of work, whose theoretical and practical frameworks fill a gap in existing literature on the subject."

—ABIODUN A. ADESEGUN, Professor of African History and History of Religious Education, Babcock University, Nigeria

"*Nkeiruka* is a remarkable contribution to African and Adventist mission historiography. Drawing on rich archival research and deep theological reflection, it reinterprets Nigerian Adventist history through the Igbo concept of *Nkeiruka*—'the future is brighter.' By weaving together stories of indigenous agency, improvisation, and resilience, the author challenges triumphalist narratives and offers a vision of mission rooted in hope and liberation. This volume not only honors the past but also gestures toward a renewed future for Adventist missiology in Africa. Thoughtful, rigorous, and profoundly contextual, *Nkeiruka* will serve as a touchstone for future scholarship in African Christian history."

—HARVEY C. KWIYANI, author of *Decolonizing Mission*

"*Nkeiruka: Critical Essays in the Mission History of Adventism in Nigeria* is a significant contribution to Adventist mission historiography in Africa. With scholarly rigor, Dr. Chigemezi Wogu situates Nigerian Adventism within wider African Christianity through the hermeneutic of *Nkeiruka*—'the future is brighter.' Moving beyond triumphalist and mere institutional narratives, he highlights indigenous agency, contextual complexity, and eschatological hope, offering a vital resource for scholars of African Christianity, mission studies, and Adventist history."

—BOUBAKAR SANOU, Chair, Department of World Mission, Andrews University, Michigan

Nkeiruka

*Critical Essays in the Mission History
of Seventh-day Adventism in Nigeria*

CHIGEMEZI NNADOZIE WOGU

Foreword by D. J. B. Trim

Preface by Gabriel Masfa

WIPF & STOCK · Eugene, Oregon

NKEIRUKA
Critical Essays in the Mission History of Seventh-day Adventism in Nigeria

Copyright © 2026 Chigemezi Nnadozie Wogu. All rights reserved. Except for brief quotations in critical publications or reviews, no part of this book may be reproduced in any manner without prior written permission from the publisher. Write: Permissions, Wipf and Stock Publishers, 199 W. 8th Ave., Suite 3, Eugene, OR 97401.

Wipf & Stock
An Imprint of Wipf and Stock Publishers
199 W. 8th Ave., Suite 3
Eugene, OR 97401

www.wipfandstock.com

PAPERBACK ISBN: 979-8-3852-5754-6
HARDCOVER ISBN: 979-8-3852-5755-3
EBOOK ISBN: 979-8-3852-5756-0

01/13/26

Chapter 2: "Trailblazers of Adventism in Nigeria, 1900s–1930s." *Journal of Adventist Mission Studies* 15 (2020) 1–13. Reused by permission from Digital Commons @ Andrews University © 2025.

Chapter 3: Adapted from John G. Nengel and Chigemezi N. Wogu, "Colonial Politics, Missionary Rivalry, and the Beginnings of Seventh-Day Adventist Mission in Northern Nigeria." *Mission Studies* 38 (2021) 213–35. Open access under a Creative Commons Attribution 4.0 International License (http://creativecommons.org/licenses/by/4.0/).

Articles in chapters 4 and 5 were originally published with *Spes Christiana*. According to the journal, the author(s) retain copyright on work published by *Spes Christiana* unless specified otherwise. Author(s) of work published by *Spes Christiana* are not required to grant *Spes Christiana* the nonexclusive unlimited rights to publish the definitive work in any format, language, and medium, for any lawful purpose. The authors retain the nonexclusive right to do anything they wish with the published article(s), provided attribution is given to *Spes Christiana* with details of the original publication, as set out in the official citation of the article published in the journal. The authors specifically have the right to post the article on the authors' or their institution's websites or in institutional or other repositories. There is no charge to authors for publishing with *Spes Christiana*.

Essay in chapter 6 was originally published with *Spectrum*. Reused and adapted by permission.

To Jijoho, my lovely wife, who seeks to understand the future,
and to Mary Adaku Wogu, my mother,
who has always seen the best that is yet to come through a
"Nkeiruka lens."

As I see what God has wrought, I am filled with astonishment, and with confidence in Christ as leader. *We have nothing to fear for the future, except as we shall forget the way the Lord has led us, and His teaching in our past history.*

Ellen G. White

Contents

Foreword by D. J. B. Trim | ix

Preface by Gabriel Masfa | xiii

Acknowledgments | xv

Introduction: *Nkeiruka*: Conception, Incubation, Birth Pains, and Birth | 1

Chapter 1: *Nkeiruka*: The Flow of Seventh-day Adventist Mission Historiography: General Adventist Mission Historiography | 7

Chapter 2: The Beginnings: Trailblazers of Adventism in Western and Southern Nigeria, 1900s–1930s | 28

Chapter 3: Colonial Politics, Missionary Rivalry, and the Beginnings of Adventist Mission in Northern Nigeria | 44

Chapter 4: The Encounter of Adventist Missionaries with Indigenous Issues in Nigeria from 1900 to the 1940s | 69

Chapter 5: Independence, Civil War, and the Beginnings of Indigenization of Adventism in Nigeria from the 1940s to 1990s | 94

Chapter 6: *Nkeiruka* and the Future of Adventism in Nigeria: Toward a Contextualized Mission History | 120

Bibliography | 137

Index | 149

Foreword
by D. J. B. Trim

CHIGEMEZI WOGU HAS DONE church historians a service by publishing this book on Nigerian Seventh-day Adventist history. There are a third of a million Adventists in Nigeria but other than Wogu's articles, gathered here (with additional chapters), there has been little scholarship on this vibrant community.[1]

Wogu has both a historical agenda and a future vision. The term *Nkeiruka*, in the important Nigerian language Igbo, means "the future is brighter"—it is both the title of this book and what might be termed its underlying argument. The book thus seeks to go beyond nostalgic reflection on the Nigerian Adventist experience, but despite its use of the upbeat "Igbo" term, the book is not a triumphalist narrative. It highlights reverses, missteps, and missed opportunities, providing a critical perspective on the past, yet in the context of an "eschatological optimism" grounded in Adventist theology, particularly its apocalyptic stress on the *parousia*. As Wogu writes, "If Adventism is the remnant church waiting for Christ's return, then history is inherently providential and hopeful."

Valuably, Wogu tells both a bottom-up and top-down story in which Adventist mission is not something simply imposed by missionaries; instead, Nigerian Adventism emerged in negotiation

---

1. There is some attention to Nigeria in Gabriel Masfa's wider synthesis, *Seventh-day Adventism in Africa*, and in my *Passion for Mission*, which is a history of the Adventist Church division that was the "parent" of work in Nigeria for nearly fifty years.

with local people and local practices. Wogu's emphasis is consistent with recent trends in Adventist historiography (chapter 1), which emphasizes local agency and adaptation. Wogu is part of a shift away from Eurocentric histories of international Adventism, exemplified by the *Encyclopedia of Seventh-day Adventists*. His attention to cultural contextualization (or the lack thereof) is particularly deep in chapter 4, but it is a theme of much of the book.

More than this, Wogu, using the work of the African historian Ogbu Kalu, calls for an African Christian historiography that is "liberative," arguing "that history must not be a neutral recounting of facts, but rather a tool that evokes critical consciousness and leads to social transformation." Wogu has done as Kalu urged, and "critically examine[d] the fundamental questions: 'why do I write, for whom and for what purpose?'" This degree of critical self-reflection is a strength of Wogu's analysis, as is the fact that it is theoretically informed, engaging with a variety of scholarship, from history to missiology to sociology. Wogu moreover uses a variety of sources, including not only Adventist periodical articles (which for some places and some periods are the only sources), but also archival sources. This adds a granularity and richness to his work, as well as making it stand out from much Adventist historiography which is solely based on published sources. He also places his work in wider historical context, again something which is not as common as it should be in Adventist histories.

Wogu shows the importance of White missionaries in Nigeria, but also reveals the role of Black and lay missionaries. For example, the first people to teach the Adventist message in Nigeria were an African American medical missionary, James Hyatt, and a Ghanaian layman, Sydney Hayford, who converted a local Nigerian, Benjamin Tikili, who joined in proselytism. Their work prompted appeals from Nigeria for ordained Adventist missionaries, which led to the arrival in the country of David Babcock and Jesse Clifford, usually said to be the first missionaries to Nigeria. Moreover, Babcock was accompanied by three African missionaries, two from Sierra Leone and one from Ghana.

FOREWORD

In chapter 3, Wogu importantly addresses the way Adventist missionaries were influenced by comity agreements, by which, around the world, different European (and, in some places, American) missionary societies or mission boards, in imperialist fashion, divided up European colonies into spheres of influence, each reserved to a particular society or board. The process by which this took place was shaped by missionaries' relations with colonial governments. The influence of comity agreements on Adventist missions is an area on which there has yet been little research, but they are known to have also affected Adventist mission growth in, for example, Papua New Guinea and East Africa. Wogu's research on this topic is groundbreaking and with implications beyond Nigeria. So, too, is his study in chapter 5 of indigenization in the forty years following World War II, which was also the period of British decolonization and Nigerian independence—and, tragically, of a massively disruptive and destructive civil war.

I do not agree with all of Dr. Wogu's interpretations, but there can be no question of the importance of his original historical research for Adventist historiography and, indeed, for wider mission historiography, with which this book is in critical dialogue. I believe it will find a wide readership.

D. J. B. TRIM
Silver Spring, Maryland

Preface
by Gabriel Masfa

THE STUDY OF CHRISTIAN missions in Africa has, in recent decades, gained fresh scholarly momentum. Yet, much of the attention has often centered on Catholic, Anglican, and Pentecostal traditions. Seventh-day Adventism, despite its global reach and its distinctive doctrinal identity, has frequently remained at the margins of Nigerian church historiography. This is why the appearance of *Critical Essays in the Mission History of Seventh-day Adventism in Nigeria* is not only timely but also pioneering. It serves as both a corrective and a contribution, drawing Adventist mission history into the wider discourse of Christianity in Africa.

This book is the product of the scholarship and dedication of Dr. Chigemezi N. Wogu, a theologian, mission historian, and scholar of world Christianity whose work continues to enrich the academy and the church alike. My relationship with Chigemezi is more than collegial; it is personal. We were classmates during our master's program at Friedensau, where our mutual interest in the history and mission of Christianity began to take shape in serious academic ways. Since then, we have supported each other's growth by sharpening each other's ideas through the mutual critique of manuscripts.

Although Wogu's main area of concentration has been in practical theology, world Christianity, and mission studies, his forays into mission history have been both groundbreaking and influential. He has opened new windows of understanding for those of us who work as church historians, showing how the

Adventist story in Nigeria intersects with broader currents of African Christianity. His painstaking research has given Adventism in Nigeria its rightful place within the landscape of mission history, ensuring that this tradition is not overlooked but recognized for its resilience, witness, and contribution to the Christian movement in Africa. For this, church historians are deeply indebted to him.

Moreover, Wogu's work complements and strengthens my own wider synthesis in Seventh-day Adventism in Africa: *A Historical Survey of the Interaction Between Religion, Traditions, and Culture*. While my study seeks to provide a continental perspective by tracing the ways Adventism has interacted with African worldviews, cultural practices, and religious traditions, his critical essays offer the depth of local narrative and detailed historical texture that enrich such a synthesis. Together, these works demonstrate that the Nigerian Adventist experience he narrates so effectively also connects with the broader story of Adventism's encounter with African societies.

Over the years, Chigemezi has rightly earned the reputation of a mission historian and missiologist, a scholar whose works demonstrate both methodological rigor and pastoral sensitivity to the lived realities of the Nigerian Adventist community. This volume reflects that dual strength—it is at once academically sound and spiritually insightful. By bringing together critical essays on Adventism in Nigeria, he has not only preserved important aspects of the past but also provided resources that will inspire future research.

The essays in this book remind us that the history of Adventism in Nigeria is not merely a denominational record but a testimony of God's leading, a witness to perseverance amid challenges, and a signpost to a hopeful future. For all these reasons, *Critical Essays in the Mission History of Seventh-day Adventism in Nigeria* stands as a remarkable achievement—one that deserves wide readership and serious engagement.

Gabriel Masfa, PhD
Nairobi, Kenya
August 28, 2025

Acknowledgments

MANY ELEMENTS AND INDIVIDUALS come together for a child to be born. This book has been born, and I must acknowledge those who made it possible.

I am so grateful to God Almighty for the grace to produce this book, especially for helping me carry the *Nkeiruka* idea for a long time. He made me see the book in the future even when it was not yet in my hands.

I thank my immediate family, Jijoho, Chimamanda, Chiedozie and Chinoye, who had to wrestle for my time during the final stages of getting this book to the publishers.

Thank you to the family of Prof. Nengel, who believed my story and helped corroborate it even though their patriarch was deceased. They helped provide the written words and permission to use Prof. Nengel's original draft in an article.

Thank you to the journal editors of *JAMS*, *Mission Studies*, *Spes Christiana*, and *Spectrum*, who implicitly supported this book by allowing some of my ideas to be published in the first place. I also thank the blind peer reviewers who, in their attempts to make any of the articles read better, inadvertently made this book read better.

Thank you to Dr. David Trim and Dr. Gabriel Masfa for agreeing to write the foreword and preface on short notice.

Thank you to Pastor John Okpechi, who helped transform the articles into a book. My profound appreciation also goes to

PREFACE

Dr. Jón Hjorleifur Stefansson, who carried out the final editorial work, ensuring that the book followed the author's style and guidelines with keen insight and meticulous attention to detail.

I appreciate the editors at Wipf and Stock who believed this book could come to fruition and for giving me additional time for its submission.

Introduction
Nkeiruka: Conception, Incubation, Birth Pains, and Birth

NKEIRUKA IS AN IGBO name given to a baby girl. Usually, the name is given on the eighth day after the birth of the baby. So, even after the child is born, the parents spend almost a week naming their offspring. This may sound like an endless time of waiting in our postmodern world. Yet, many Igbos still practice the tradition. But when a child is named Nkeiruka ("the future is bright," or "the best is yet to come"), serious reflection must have transpired for the name to come to light. From the time of conceiving the idea to the time it takes to ruminate over possible names that carry the idea and to finally naming the child, Igbos consciously take their time for a child's name to be "born."

This volume has taken time to be born. In fact, it has been in a long incubation stage. It was first conceived around 2016/17 when I began seriously thinking about the lack of a serious mission historiographical reflection related to Adventist mission history in Nigeria. By that time, I was already deep into my doctoral thesis at Vrije Universiteit, Amsterdam, while already halfway into the research management and writing of key articles for the *Encyclopedia of Seventh-day Adventists* (*ESDA*) office in Europe. Both the doctoral research and the work for *ESDA* served as gunpowder for the initial stages of conceiving this book. Through *ESDA* and the magnanimity of my bosses Stefan Höschele, Daniel Heinz, and

David Trim, while accessing historical data for the *ESDA* project, I could also use the time to hunt historical documents pertaining to Nigeria. General Conference archives in the United States and the European Adventist archives in Germany were instrumental in this.

The conception stage gave into the incubation stage when I began publishing articles about Adventist mission history in Nigeria. It began with writing "Trailblazers of Adventism in Nigeria, 1900s–1930s," which was published with *Journal of Adventist Mission Studies* in 2020. The next year Brill's *Mission Studies* accepted to publish the coauthored article "Colonial Politics, Missionary Rivalry, and the Beginnings of Seventh-Day Adventist Mission in Northern Nigeria." This article was born after I had visited the North of Nigeria and eventually met with the late Professor John Garah Nengel, professor emeritus of history, University of Jos, Nigeria. He had written a purely archival historical account of Adventism in the North of Nigeria. Yet he offered that I take the work, brush it up, and publish as I wished. Unfortunately, he died before the article was published. Still, I would not have been able to make the arguments made in this book without Professor Nengel's rigorous archival draft. *Spes Christiana*, the journal of European Adventist Society of Theology and Religious Studies, published two of my articles in 2020 and 2023. The first was "Preparing Converts for the second coming of Christ: The Encounter of Seventh-day Adventist Missionaries with Indigenous Issues in Nigeria from 1900 to the 1940s" and the second was "Independence, Civil War, and the Beginnings of Indigenization of Seventh-day Adventism in Nigeria from the 1940s to 1990s."

By the time I had published those four articles, I began entering the stage of birth pangs. This was the stage where I knew I needed to put all the articles together as a book. However, no publisher (Adventist and non-Adventist) was willing to assist in giving birth to this book, *Nkeiruka*. It was also at this time that I wrote a draft of the last chapter for the Adventist *Spectrum Magazine* in 2023: "Nigerian Adventism: History and Promise."

INTRODUCTION

It was not until Wipf and Stock agreed to hold my hands that I finally was able to push the final stages to birth this book. All the articles mentioned above form the core of this book. Apart from the first chapter, those essays have now been combined in this volume. It is with a heart of thanks to the editors of *JAMS*, *Mission Studies*, *Spes Christiana*, and *Spectrum* that I now introduce the approach of this book.

The core argument or leitmotif of this book is embedded in the Igbo concept of *Nkeiruka*, meaning "the future is brighter." It serves as a potent historiographical metaphor for understanding Adventist mission history, advocating a deliberate shift from nostalgic recollections and institutional memory towards critical reflection and anticipatory vision. This framework interprets history through a lens of "eschatological optimism," an Adventist core epistemology, where the promise of Christ's second coming shapes the narrative. This book argues for an intentional approach to mission history in Africa, moving beyond simple chronology to focus on liberation and hope. This perspective allows for the integration of suffering and setbacks into a larger story of progress and redemption. The book integrates some of Ogbu Kalu's ideas about understanding the history of the church in Africa but departs from his ecumenical approach. Unlike Kalu's focus on interdenominational relations, this book is more confessional and emphasizes Adventism's unique, hope-filled journey into the future.

The overarching question of this book is this: How can the concept of *Nkeiruka* ground an inquiry on the flow of Adventist mission historiography in Nigeria? To answer this question, the historical data contained in this book has been gathered from both serious archival and library research, review of historical documents and mission history ethnography, and a few oral interviews.

Thus, this book makes a serious historiographical call. Instead of portraying the global spread of Adventism as the result of a seamless, top-down strategic plan, the mission history that the reader is confronted with highlights:

1. Moments of uncertainty, improvisation, and failure in mission work.
2. Critical decisions by local leaders and missionaries who navigated resistance, adapted doctrine to context, or prioritized education/health care over direct proselytization.
3. Missed opportunities and alternative models of growth that were discarded or marginalized.

For example, Nigerian Adventism did not emerge uniformly. The church grew unevenly, and often despite, not because of, central mission policy. This was due to local adaptations, tensions with colonial structures, and indigenous agency.

Thus, chapter 2 is written with a view to demonstrate that mission historiography can foreground the individual and collective choices of those on the margins of the mission structure. These can include teachers who opened schools without formal church sanction. It does not exempt indigenous leaders who reinterpreted eschatology or Sabbath-keeping in culturally meaningful ways. Further, it reconsiders converts who maintained dual identities or merged Adventist faith with ethnic traditions. Therefore, rather than treating these figures as exceptions, they become central to how Adventism took root often through negotiation, not transplantation.

In chapters 3 and 4, the role of language, local customs, and existing religious dynamics in shaping how Adventist beliefs were presented is problematized. Especially in chapter 3, I explore how political shifts, such as colonial policies, forced missionaries to rethink or localize their approaches. For example, in Northern Nigeria, Adventist growth was constrained not just by colonial resistance but by strategic missteps in cultural engagement, unlike more nimble approaches seen elsewhere.

In chapter 5, while dealing with issues like nationhood and faith, civil war and campus revivals, the chapter demonstrates the effects of post-independence nationalism on mission and indigenization of Adventism in Nigeria. Ultimately, the emergence of vernacular faith expressions of Adventism was shaped more by context than by the top-down administrative policy and vision.

Finally, chapter 6 contextualizes the insights from chapters 1 to 5 to speak about the future of Adventist mission history.

It is my hope that mission historians can benefit from this volume by noting that "life can only be understood backwards, but it must be lived forwards" (Søren Kierkegaard) because the future is brighter than we can imagine.

Let me end this introduction with the words of Ellen G. White who implicitly encouraged us to not be worried about the future because the Lord has led us well in the past:

> In reviewing our past history, having traveled over every step of advance to our present standing, I can say, Praise God! As I see what God has wrought, I am filled with astonishment, and with confidence in Christ as leader. *We have nothing to fear for the future, except as we shall forget the way the Lord has led us, and His teaching in our past history.*[1]

Nkeiruka!

---

1. White, *Life Sketches*, 196. Emphasis added.

Chapter 1

Nkeiruka: The Flow of Seventh-day Adventist Mission Historiography

General Adventist Mission Historiography

A CAUSAL REFLECTION INTO Adventist mission historiography reveals some clear historical patterns of expansion and underlying theological backgrounds. Among key scholars[1] the global Adventist mission historiography has evolved through identifiable phases, reflecting changing theological emphases while entering intercultural contexts. This underscores that mission is not merely an activity but a fundamental theological driver that shapes how Adventists construct and understand their own history.

For instance, in the early Millerite period (1840s), Adventists viewed themselves as God's remnant awaiting Christ's return. After the Great Disappointment of 1844, a "shut-door" theology prevailed: Outreach was largely internal (to former Millerites) and evangelistic activity among outsiders was de-emphasized. Mission

---

1. Oosterwal, *Mission: Possible*; Oliver, "Principles for Reorganization"; Höschele, *From the End of the World*.

was understood as preserving the faithful until Christ's coming, not as sending others out.

Soon, as scholars note, there was a critical shift from "shut-door" to "open-door" missiology. By the late 1840s and early 1850s, the "shut-door" theory was abandoned, marking a new period in Adventist missiology. This shift was driven by new theological understandings, such as the sealing of God's people still being in the future (implying Rev 7 had not yet begun), and empirical realities, including non-Millerites joining the Sabbatarian Adventists.

Sabbatarian Adventists began focusing on calling other Protestants to join the Adventist movement. In practice, this meant forming formal structures: In 1863, the denomination organized the General Conference to coordinate preaching and education.

One must note that using the "Great Disappointment" and infusing the term "shut-door" is an iterative process of historiographical reinterpretation. It has become a pattern of how Adventist historians narrate and justify their missiological advance in history. Looking back to reinterpret the Disappointment of 1844 was not merely acknowledging a theological setback but a profound way of recognizing a historiographical crucible. Looking back to see that there was a shift to an open-door era signifies a shift in Adventist self-narrative from a restrictive, exclusive "remnant" (confined to a specific group of Millerites) to one with a universal mandate.

This development has directly impacted how Adventists understand their past mission history. The "shut-door" period was a phase of limited understanding of their mission while the "open-door" demonstrates their future trajectory, that of a global mission, indicating how theological development directly shapes and reshapes historical narrative.

Yet, even with global vision, there seems to have been a shift in focus as historians look back to the period of 1888 to the 1930s. For instance, the 1888 General Conference in Minneapolis marked a major theological shift as Ellet J. Waggoner and Alonzo T. Jones urged that Adventist doctrines be centered on the gospel, righteousness by faith. Their message was eventually embraced, leading to renewed focus on Protestant theology and a closer alignment of Adventist identity with the Christian gospel and evangelical tradition.

This singular event became a historiographical watershed in reevaluating Adventist theological distinctives and mission. The 1888 session was not merely a theological event; it was a historiographical refounding of the denomination's self-understanding.

This paradigm shift ushered Adventism into what many have referred to as the golden age of Adventist mission. In this era or phase, leaders like Arthur G. Daniells and William A. Spicer centralized and expanded the church's mission efforts. In 1901, Daniells reorganized church governance into Union Conferences and launched the "springboard plan," where each mission field became self-supporting and a base for further outreach. Missionary work rapidly intensified across cultures and continents. Revelation 14:6 was now seen as a literal global mandate to prepare the world for Christ's return.[2]

Reflecting on how Adventist mission history has been written, scholars note a shift from devotional narrative to critical scholarship. Early Adventist histories (e.g., Ellen White, Uriah Smith, A. T. Jones) were not just *apologetic*, I would say, but triumphalist, using history to illustrate divine providence rather than to critique the past. They often borrowed Protestant historical accounts to bolster theology (White famously paraphrased Jean-Henri Merle d'Aubigné and others). Only in the mid-twentieth century did Adventist historiography professionalize. Researchers like George Knight and Daniel McAdams have documented this maturation: By the late twentieth century "professionally trained historians" began applying critical methods and engaging secular history alongside church records.[3]

Scholars like Gottfried Oosterwal exemplified the transition from apologetic storytelling to a more analytical, interdisciplinary historiography where data collection and evaluation were advocated to show the "participation in Christ's own mission" as

2. Wogu, "Development of Adventist Missiology."
3. Reynaud, "Understanding History."

the central organizing principle of church life.[4] Here Adventist mission history was entering into a critical renewal phase where themes like adaptation, diversity, and new frontiers began playing key roles in the historicity of Adventist mission agenda. At the juncture from triumphalist historiography to critical renewal, we find historical theologian Pieter Gerard Damsteegt.

In the classic *The Foundation of the Seventh-Day Adventist Message and Mission* (1977), Damsteegt combined meticulous archival research with a confessional focus, tracing how Adventist doctrines (Sabbath, sanctuary, prophetic expectation) directly shaped early mission strategies. By systematizing the doctrinal underpinnings of mission, Damsteegt laid crucial groundwork by providing the raw material and critical questions that later scholars would use to reexamine through broader cultural, postcolonial, and multi-voice lenses. Damsteegt stands as the theological-historical bridge between the church's mid-century self-definition and the post-2000 historiographical renewal.[5]

Here, and almost in the same spirit, Stefan Höschele's claims are instructive. He has argued that one can gain better insights if theological, strategical, and practical dimensions of Adventist mission are compared particularly with the evangelical movement. Höschele's comparative method is crucial for a nuanced historiography of this period. By juxtaposing Adventist mission with evangelicalism, it becomes clear that the post-1888 shift was not merely an internal theological adjustment but also a strategic alignment with a broader Protestant tradition.[6] Based on the above, it is no wonder that the Adventist revisionist historian Goerge K. Knight called mission history development a "search for identity."[7]

With the postwar expansion and rise of indigenous churches in countries where Adventism had entered, we see a shift in Adventist mission historiography. Calls arose for a radical reinterpretation of the "remnant" concept. This showcases a profound

---

4. Oosterwal, *Mission: Possible*.
5. Damsteegt, *Foundations*.
6. Höschele, *From the End of the World*.
7. Knight, "Adventist Theology 1844 to 1994."

historiographical shift from an exclusive, sectarian self-identity to an inclusive, universal vision. This evolution directly challenges earlier, narrower historical narratives of Adventist uniqueness, forcing a reevaluation of their historical relationship with other faiths and their own place in global religious history. It signifies a move towards a more sophisticated, less triumphalist historiography that grapples with religious pluralism and the idea of God's work beyond denominational boundaries.

While this may seem like a historiographical jump, Gabriel Masfa's 2021 work represents a further deepening of the post-2000 "historiographical renewal." In his *Seventh-day Adventist Historiography*, Masfa departs from purely chronological surveys and instead explores how Adventist historians worldwide have approached core themes such as mission, prophecy, and enculturation. By so doing, Masfa contributes to an Adventist mission historiography that decenters Western narratives. He extends Damsteegt's theological-historical bridge. More so, he explicitly asks how "faith" and "history" interact in Adventist scholarship, offering a nuanced historiographical model that integrates rigorous source criticism with an openness to the community's belief commitments.[8]

With the involvement of more scholars, non-Western and postcolonial voices, and the aims of the *Encyclopedia of Seventh-day Adventism* (*ESDA*), Adventist mission historiography is no longer in the stage of search for identity where theological focus in various eras helped interpret Adventist mission. Rather, it is now in the stage of identity portrayal. It marks a shift to a critical historiography of mission that subjects mission-history accounts to fresh critical methods, archival reappraisals, and the digital synthesis espoused by *ESDA*. David Trim's recent *Hearts of Faith* foregrounds this critical approach. His work centers on the fundamental nineteen-year period between the Great Disappointment of 1844 and the formal emergence of the Seventh-day Adventist Church in 1863. Rather than portraying the church's rise as preordained, Trim argues that its establishment hinged on the *choices*

---

8. Masfa, *Seventh-Day Adventist Historiography*.

made by early believers during that transitional era. He concludes that different paths were truly possible.⁹ This perspective invites mission historians to similarly reconsider the often-implied inevitability of global Adventist mission expansion. How might mission history be reframed if we focused not just on institutional momentum but on contingent decisions, risk-taking individuals, and contextual strategy in the field?

In my own work, I have exemplified this trend using academic models (drawing on Höschele's comparative missiology) and recognizing the need for multidisciplinary methods. Nonetheless, Adventist mission historiography remains underdeveloped (in "infant stages" of reflection) and the scholarship is still influenced by Global North perspectives. That is why my call for incorporating religious studies, sociology, and local theology tools remains. This call echoes a broader move in church history toward diverse methodologies.¹⁰

Adventist historiography has evolved from a largely internal, often apologetic method (focused on explaining and defending distinctives) to a more sophisticated, critical, and comparative approach. It signifies a move towards academic rigor and a willingness to confront complex historical realities, rather than simply affirming a predetermined or idealized narrative. This maturation enhances the depth and credibility of Adventist historical understanding.

The overall progression reflects a fundamental paradigm shift in Adventist historical self-perception: from a defensive, identity-confirming historiography, primarily focused on internal distinctives and survival, to a more adaptive, outward-looking one. This involves a continuous reinterpretation of foundational events and concepts to maintain relevance and effectiveness in a rapidly changing global landscape. This shift demonstrates a growing maturity in how Adventists understand their place in broader history and their ongoing mission.

Before turning to Africa, it is important to make a few comments on Adventist mission historiography in Europe, South America, and Asia.

9. Trim, *Hearts of Faith*.
10. Wogu, "Development of Adventist Missiology."

European scholarship on Seventh-day Adventism has shifted from a focus on key figures[11] to an emphasis on local adaptation.[12] Recent studies like *Parochialism, Pluralism, and Contextualization*, as well as *Contours of European Adventism*, analyze how doctrines were received and reshaped within German, French, and Slavic cultures. They reveal significant internal debates, divergent leadership, and contingent outcomes, not just top-down momentum. These works examine how the church in Europe negotiated secularism and national identity,[13] demonstrating that mission history has been shaped by how local leaders actively questioned inherited mission models, sometimes diverging from official strategy. In essence, mission historiography in Europe shows that the church's regional development was shaped by local decisions and contextual interactions.

In Latin America, classical studies done by Floyd Greenleaf emphasize how the "delay" of the second Advent and adaptation to indigenous cultures led Adventism to develop schools, hospitals, and publishing houses. His two-volume set and subsequent work on South America provide a comprehensive institutional history of the church's expansion.[14] This approach, which is also demonstrated in other works,[15] represents a classic, top-down perspective, detailing the growth of the organization and its administrative structures. The recent *Foundational Missionaries of South American Adventism* showcases evidence of beginning to rethink Adventist mission history. Yet, mission historiography is still at a developmental stage for that region.

Asia parallels some trends from Latin American in the historiography of Seventh-day Adventist missions, especially focusing on the missionaries and history of denominational structures. Yet

---

11. See, e.g., Heinz, *Ludwig Richard Conradi*; Greenleaf, *Church, State, and Religious Dissent*.

12. Hartlapp, *Siebenten-Tags-Adventisten im Nationalsozialismus*.

13. Trim and Heinz, *Parochialism, Pluralism, and Contextualization*; Höschele and Wogu, *Contours of European Adventism*.

14. Greenleaf, *Land of Hope*; Greenleaf, *Seventh-day Adventist Church*.

15. See, e.g., O'Reggio, "Early Adventist Mission to Jamaica."

it has undergone a marked shift toward certifying local agency. A prime example is Tadaomi Shinmyo's missiological history of Japan where the slow, uneven growth of the church is explained less by doctrinal deficiency than by shifting political, religious, and secular pressures.[16] Another example is Christie Chui-Shan Chow's *Schism: Seventh-day Adventism in Post-Denominational China*. The historical and ethnographical monograph documents how Chinese Adventists endured split factions under the Three-Self Patriotic Movement but ultimately preserved a self-conscious denominational identity through grassroots networks, kinship ties, and the translation or publication of Ellen White's writings.[17]

From this short overview, one can say that Adventist mission historiography in Europe, South America, and Asia is evolving from a traditional, top-down approach that focuses on key figures and institutional growth. New scholarship in Europe and Asia increasingly emphasizes local adaptation, grassroots agency, and the contingent cultural and political factors that shaped the church's development. We now turn to Africa.

ADVENTIST MISSION HISTORIOGRAPHY IN AFRICA

In the mission historiography of Adventism in Africa, there appears to be a more nuanced focus on different phases: from the establishment and mission story era to expansion and institutionalization during the colonial period, and finally to indigenous initiatives in the postcolonial and contemporary era. In the mission story era, hagiographical narratives often spoke about the establishment of Adventist mission in various countries or regions by the efforts of missionaries. The years of the 1860s to the early 1900s always praised the pioneering efforts of missionaries. To a varying extent, this kind of reading of Adventism in Africa remains widely acknowledged.

---

16. Shinmyo, "History in Missiological Perspective."
17. Chow, *Schism*.

Then came the era of expansion and institutionalization from the early 1900s until the 1940s. While not so much different from the previous era, its focus was no longer the pioneering efforts of colonial mission structure, but the inroads and success of how a denomination became institutionalized in Africa. Here too, the focus was on foreign agency.

After many African countries began gaining independence from their colonial masters, the gradual handover of the African church to indigenous leaders began. Consequently, this era saw the rise of indigenous historians who did not really question the mission stories or the institutionalization era but told Adventist mission history from an indigenous perspective, highlighting also the challenges of the African church.

Then came the postcolonial phase of reinterpretation of Adventism in Africa. It is a kind of revisionist agenda that began asking critical questions that emerged from early missionary stories, using missionary ethnography and applying sociological and anthropological approaches to show that early Adventist inroads into Africa were characterized by a blend of individual pioneering efforts, often through literature and indigenous converts, preceding formal missionary arrivals.

This organic, "bottom-up" propagation, combined with a holistic mission strategy that integrated evangelism with institutional development in education and healthcare, proved highly effective in establishing a strong presence across the continent. The colonial era saw the institutionalization of Adventism in Africa, marked by significant organizational growth and the establishment of regional divisions, even amidst challenges from colonial authorities, other denominations, and the harsh environment.[18]

The postcolonial phase in Adventist mission historiography in Africa also marks a shift from depending on missionaries as the heroes of Adventism to critically asking why some beliefs have stayed and become ingrained in Adventism in Africa. It is an era that studies the inheritance and innovation of Adventism in Africa.

18. Masfa, *Seventh-Day Adventism in Africa*.

This era has shown that the postcolonial period brought new complexities, notably the Africanization of leadership and the ongoing struggle for financial self-sufficiency. While the church in Africa has experienced phenomenal growth, becoming a leading center of global Adventism, it continues to navigate deep-seated cultural issues such as polygamy, dual allegiance, and spiritualistic manifestations, requiring nuanced contextualization and the development of relevant healing ministries. The emergence of "reverse mission," with African Adventists serving as missionaries in the Global North, signifies a profound shift in global mission dynamics, challenging traditional paradigms and highlighting the interconnectedness of the worldwide church.[19]

Despite its remarkable growth and adaptability, Adventist missiological thinking in Africa continues to evolve, with ongoing needs for deeper theological reflection on its unique challenges and opportunities. The future flow of Adventist mission historiography in Africa will undoubtedly be shaped by its ability to foster indigenous theological production, embrace local "Adventisms," and develop strategies that authentically address the spiritual, social, and cultural realities of the continent, ensuring continued relevance and growth in a rapidly changing world.

DEALING WITH THE WHY OR THE NEED FOR A HISTORIOGRAPHICAL REFLECTION IN ADVENTIST MISSION HISTORY IN NIGERIA (AFRICA)

There is a great need for a critical historiographical reflection of Adventist mission history in Africa. This need is embedded in the question "Why?" When mission historians begin grappling with the *why*, they can understand why certain narratives are emphasized, whose voices are omitted, and what interpretive frameworks are used. This lack of reflection is particularly striking given for

---

19. Masfa, *Seventh-Day Adventism in Africa*; see chapter 8 in Masfa's book where he attempts to portray the issues as an identity crisis.

instance Nigeria's own rich historiographical traditions and the parallel development of postcolonial theological scholarship across African Christianity.

My suggestion is to do this via the lens of *Nkeiruka*.

The term *Nkeiruka* has been drawn from Igbo language and spirituality. It is translated as "the future is brighter." This theme is deeply resonant within Nigeria's (African) eschatological thought. *Nkeiruka* offers a compelling framework to examine the historiography of Seventh-day Adventism in Nigeria. It is positioned at the intersection of theological imagination and historical methodology. Hence, the term serves as a historiographical metaphor because it argues for a shift from nostalgia and institutional memory to critical reflection and anticipatory vision.

By taking this term into historiography and inviting the late African scholar and historian Ogbu Kalu into the conversation, Adventist mission history is not treated merely as a record of events, but as a narrative in motion. Adventist mission history becomes one that reflects the theological core of Adventism (expectation of the parousia) and responds dynamically to the sociopolitical contexts of Nigerian (African) history. Thus, instead of a backward-looking perspective on the past best times, we need a forward-looking perspective to critically reflect on Adventist mission historiography.

OGBU KALU AND THE FLOW OF AFRICAN CHURCH HISTORIOGRAPHY

In the introductory chapter of *African Christianity: An African Story*, Ogbu Kalu provides church historians with a prolegomenon in African mission historiography.[20] His essay challenges the academic community to move beyond archival missionary histories. Instead, mission historians are to craft theological, contextual, and people-driven accounts of the acts of God in Africa that reflect the hybrid, dynamic, and Spirit-infused character of African Christianity.

---

20. Kalu, "Shape and Flow."

Kalu begins with a call to reanimate historical memory in African Christian communities, situating African church historiography as a liberative enterprise. He argues that history must not be a neutral recounting of facts, but rather a tool that evokes critical consciousness and leads to social transformation. Using African proverbs and the reflections of thinkers like Henri Marrou and Eduardo Hoornaert, Kalu frames the historian as a prophetic figure. For Kalu, the historian is someone dispatched to bridge past and present in service of Africa's future.[21]

This perspective compels the historian to critically examine the fundamental questions: "Why do I write, for whom and for what purpose?"[22]

In making his point, Kalu identifies four major concerns shaping modern African church historiography. The first deals with continuity with African primal religion. Kalu argues that Christianity in Africa must be understood not as a foreign transplant but as growing out of the soil of African religious consciousness. Thus, in this assessment, African worldviews, symbols, and rituals provide a conceptual framework for interpreting the Christian message. Scholars like Kwame Bediako and Andrew Walls argue that African Christianity continues the narrative of African religion while also expanding the story of global Christianity.[23]

Secondly, Kalu argues for a Christocentric and theological approach, viewing the church as a spiritual body on a mission, grounded in eschatological hope and a prophetic concern for justice. Thirdly, he mentions a crucial shift from a missionary history that depicted Africans as passive recipients to an ecumenical historiography that elevates African voices and recognizes their agency. Furthermore, this history must actively engage with public life. This fourth concern sees Christianity as a mission to culture

---

21. The historian is a "missionary dispatched to the past to strike a hyphen between the past and the present." Here, Kalu is quoting Henri Marou. "Shape and Flow," 1.

22. Kalu, "Shape and Flow," 1.

23. Kalu, "Shape and Flow," 2–3. See Bediako, *Christianity in Africa*; Walls and Fyfe, *Christianity in Africa*.

that addresses pressing sociopolitical issues like poverty and corruption. Here, the "memory of the people of God"[24] serves as a powerful tool for resisting oppression and affirming human dignity. Ultimately, African church history should be a vibrant narrative that reflects its unique spiritual, social, and political dimensions.

Kalu defines church history as a theological and political discipline which must move beyond institutional records and missionary reports to reflect the lived faith of people. Drawing on biblical concepts of the church as *ekklesia* (a called-out people), Kalu emphasizes that church history is about God's activity among the poor and the marginalized, and how African communities have responded to the divine in their cultural and historical settings.[25] He critiques traditional models of church history. For instance, institutional historiography focuses on denominational expansion and organizational milestones but often ignores grassroots spirituality and African agency.[26]

Further, missionary historiography is unfortunately often triumphalist, Eurocentric, and dismissive of indigenous religious heritage, portraying missionaries as heroic civilizers and fails to see Africans as active participants.[27] On the other hand, nationalist historiography seeks to reclaim African Christian agency but sometimes overcorrects by blaming all colonial-era failures on missionaries while overlooking the complex role of African intermediaries (catechists, elders, converts, etc.).[28]

Finally, Kalu critiques sociological and anthropological approaches to African church history for focusing too heavily on outward, secular effects like social and economic change. He argues that this often overlooks the internal, spiritual dimensions of faith central to African Christianity. Citing Lamin Sanneh, Kalu

---

24. Kalu, "Shape and Flow," 2.
25. Kalu, "Shape and Flow," 9.
26. Kalu, "Shape and Flow," 14–15.
27. Kalu, "Shape and Flow," 15–16. E.g., Dodds, *Ibo Opening*.
28. Kalu, "Shape and Flow," 17. Here we see the works of Ajayi, *Christian Missions in Nigeria*, and Ayandele, *Missionary Impact on Modern Nigeria*.

calls for a more holistic approach that honors both the social and deeply religious aspects of Christian experience.[29]

In this vein, Kalu argues for a people-centered, contextual, and theological historiography, one that tells the story "from below," through the experiences of real communities struggling with modernity, tradition, and transformation.[30]

In a similar vein, the Igbo concept of *Nkeiruka*, meaning "the future is brighter," serves as a potent historiographical metaphor for understanding Adventist mission history, advocating a deliberate shift from nostalgic recollections and institutional memory towards critical reflection and an anticipatory vision.

This book integrates some of the ideas of Ogbu Kalu. It is on this premise that this book has been written arguing that mission history must be approached with intentionality, a clear purpose, and an unwavering commitment to liberation and future hope, moving beyond simple chronology or self-congratulatory institutional accounts. The very act of writing history in the African context is inherently performative, actively shaping social consciousness and collective identity. This suggests that historiography carries a profound ethical responsibility to serve truth and liberation, rather than merely documenting facts.

Furthermore, the integration of eschatological thought provides a unique lens through which to interpret historical developments. This is where this book departs especially from Kalu's ecumenical approach. Kalu's ecumenical approach to African Christian history foregrounds the plurality of Christian expressions and emphasizes interdenominational interactions, especially in how African Independent Churches, Pentecostals, and mission-founded denominations shape each other's development. In contrast, this volume is more confessional and inward-facing, reflecting on Seventh-day Adventism's distinct theological identity and its future within African contexts, rather than emphasizing cross-denominational entanglements. Whereas Kalu's

---

29. Kalu, "Shape and Flow," 18–21. Here of course, the work of Sanneh, *West African Christianity*.

30. Kalu, "Shape and Flow," 22.

historiography celebrates the shared African Christian story, this volume frames Adventist mission as a hope-filled, denominationally bounded journey into the future.

The *Nkeiruka* concept directly links the Igbo phrase "the future is brighter" to the "eschatological optimism" inherent in Adventism, particularly its expectation of the parousia (Christ's second coming). This is not merely a theological belief that exists within the historical narrative, but a powerful framework for interpreting the history itself. It suggests that even periods of profound suffering, conflict, or apparent setbacks can be integrated into a larger narrative of progress and redemption. This forward-looking and hopeful approach challenges static or purely retrospective historical accounts, encouraging a perspective that sees divine purpose unfolding even amidst human struggles. The question is, how can *Nkeiruka* ground an inquiry on the flow of Adventist mission historiography in Nigeria? The next section delves into this.

NKEIRUKA AND THE FLOW OF SEVENTH-DAY ADVENTIST MISSION HISTORIOGRAPHY

Among the Igbos of Nigeria, *Nkeiruka* is a female name. Naming can be influenced by several factors such as personal experiences or the circumstances surrounding the birth of a child. It may also be based on the religious leanings of the parents.[31] Igbos "do not give names to their children randomly. The names they give their children have social, linguistic, historical, religious, and philosophic connotations."[32] Names and "naming of Igbo children are a projection of not only the whims of the parents but also a window through which we mirror their lives and concatenations."[33] Therefore when a girl child is named *Nkeiruka*, the name instills a future-oriented, optimistic, and divinely guided perspective from

---

31. Ezenwafor-Afuecheta and Onyeocha, "Dynamics of Name-Taking."
32. Cookey and Ijioma, "Panoramic Study of Names," 21.
33. Cookey and Ijioma, "Panoramic Study of Names," 21.

an early age, making the philosophy a lived reality and the name itself a cultural anchor for its principles.[34]

Interestingly, the name *Nkeiruka* can be contrasted with another name, *Azubuike*, which means "your past is your strength." Unlike *Azubuike* which is backward-looking, *Nkeiruka* is forward-looking. In fact, beyond naming, *Nkeiruka* is a theory of hope.[35] It is a philosophy of hope rooted in Igbo wisdom, symbolized by the tireless hen that persists through life's struggles with the belief that the future holds greater promise. It encourages hard work, resilience, and vigilance despite present challenges. The idea underscores the existential value of giving meaning to life through perseverance rather than surrendering to despair. By engaging life's hardships, one discovers purpose and fulfillment.[36]

The *Nkeiruka* concept embodies a cultural epistemology that emphasizes hope, resilience, and the belief in a better tomorrow. It serves as a metaphor to transcend past challenges and negative vicissitudes of mission history to focus on the possibilities of the future of the mission of God. This forward-looking perspective promotes a belief of optimism, suggesting that despite present uncertainties faced by Adventism, the future holds potential for progress.

Seventh-day Adventist theology is deeply rooted in an eschatological optimism centered on the expectation of the parousia, the second coming of Christ. This belief positions the parousia as the grand climax of the gospel, where sin, pain, and sorrows cease, the righteous are resurrected and taken to heaven, and the unrighteous are judged. Adventists view this event as the fulfillment of God's promises and the beginning of a new era of peace and justice.[37] This eschatological hope shapes their worldview, mission, and ethical conduct, emphasizing the importance of living in anticipation of Christ's return and the establishment of God's kingdom on

---

34. Igwe, "Nkeiruka."
35. Igwe, "Nkeiruka."
36. Igwe, "Nkeiruka."
37. General Conference of Seventh-day Adventists, *Seventh-day Adventists Believe*, 371–85.

earth. As Jon Paulien[38] would argue, "being an Adventist is to have a sense of prophetic destiny [prophetic future] . . . [that works to] restore things that have been lost and reconcile people who have been at odds with each other for many centuries."[39]

Both *Nkeiruka* and Adventist eschatological optimism share a common epistemological framework that emphasizes a forward-looking hope. While *Nkeiruka* is rooted in Igbo cultural identity and history, and Adventist optimism is grounded in Christian theology, both perspectives encourage mission historians to transcend past difficulties and present worries to focus on the potential of the future. This shared outlook fosters a sense of historiographical resilience motivating historians to engage the past actively in shaping a better future.

NKEIRUKA AS AN ADVENTIST EPISTEMOLOGY OF MISSION HISTORY

In the following, I posit that mission historians should embrace *Nkeiruka* as an epistemological motif—a lens through which to understand mission history. If Adventism is the remnant church waiting for Christ's return, then history is inherently providential and hopeful. *Nkeiruka* resonates with Adventist eschatological optimism. Even when missions seemed to falter, the denomination believed the future held blessing. In historiographical terms, this means writing with an orientation to progress and redemption. For example, when chronicling controversies or setbacks (such as the Northern Nigerian crisis of the 1980s or debates over African traditional religions), a *Nkeiruka* perspective would underscore how these challenges can eventually lead to growth or new opportunities. In Adventist historiography this inspires narratives that integrate suffering and victory.

Moreover, *Nkeiruka* informs the way Adventists interpret God's moving among nations. Instead of nostalgia for a pristine

---

38. Paulien, "Best Is Yet to Come."
39. Paulien, "Best Is Yet to Come," 39.

"golden age" of missions, historians influenced by this epistemology look for ongoing continuities of mission promise. Just as the hen in the Igbo worldview works tirelessly for her chicks without immediate reward, Adventists see their own trailblazers laboring in faith with trust that the harvest will come. Thus, even seemingly minor figures (a local evangelist, a schoolteacher) are portrayed as heirs of *Nkeiruka*—people whose labors point to a brighter future for the church. This aligns with Damsteegt's note that Adventists came to view themselves as "co-workers with Christ,"[40] or as active participants in God's unfolding mission. These suggestions are possible within two theological frameworks: *missio Dei* and *motus Dei*.

Missio Dei and *Motus Dei*

Missio Dei ("the mission of God") emphasizes that mission originates from God, not from institutional structures or colonial mandates. David J. Bosch's famous quote, "Mission is not primarily an activity of the church, but an attribute of God. God is a missionary God,"[41] underscores the idea that even though a church sends a missionary from point A to B, it was God working in the shadows. Thus, before a mission board sat to plan about a country, God had already taken the initiative in that local context. *Missio Dei* echoes the concept of *Nkeiruka*, which trusts in a future made brighter by divine initiative rather than merely human ambition. In both, hope is not passive but actively shaped by grace and human response.

Motus Dei ("the movement of God") complements *missio Dei* by suggesting that divine action often occurs outside institutional control through revivals, grassroots movements, or subaltern spiritualities. A *motus Dei* framework shows that the "God of the Bible is continually on the move and as one who beckons his followers to come alongside to see what God is doing in the world. Thus, the mission is about moving with God to see all things made new as we harmonize our wandering steps to be in sync with a

---

40. Damsteegt, "Foundations," 3–18.
41. Bosch, *Transforming Mission*, 389–90.

moving God."[42] *Motus Dei* resonates with *Nkeiruka*'s metaphor of resilience trusting that persistence and divine momentum will bring growth and fulfillment, even amid uncertainty.

When *missio Dei* and *motus Dei* are applied historiographically, mission historians are challenged to center mission as divine initiative and local response, not just missionary logistics. This becomes a hermeneutic for writing Adventist history that recognizes providential patterns and divine movement as well as shifting emphasis to the spontaneous movements of the Spirit and indigenous initiatives that are often central to the spread of faith in the spread of Adventism. By so doing, reductionist mission narratives that equate mission history with foreign initiative is problematized. Moreover, these theological concepts allow us to hold in tension both human failure and divine possibility, a duality that lies at the heart of this mission historiographical journey.

Having explored the various concepts, the question is how the insights from Ogbu Kalu amalgamated with the concept of *Nkeiruka* under the theological theme of *missio Dei* and *motus Dei* play out in the mission historiography of Adventism in Nigeria.

THE NEED FOR A CRITICAL HISTORIOGRAPHICAL REFLECTION IN AFRICAN (NIGERIAN) ADVENTISM

As will be shown in the chapters that follow, the historiography of Adventism in Nigeria has remained largely institutional, often echoing the narratives of Western mission reports, sanitized denominational publications, and internal celebratory accounts. Early writings tended to prioritize the lives of foreign missionaries, the growth of church membership, and the establishment of mission schools and hospitals. These were often framed in the "triumphalist" register typical of colonial-era mission historiography.

What is missing is a deep historiographical reflection. This reflection centers on grappling with *why* certain narratives are

---

42. George and Harold, "Motus Dei (The Move of God)," 1–12.

emphasized, whose voices are omitted, and what interpretive frameworks are used. This lack of reflection is particularly striking given Nigeria's own rich historiographical traditions and the parallel development of postcolonial theological scholarship across African Christianity. Thus, the reader would notice that this book approaches Adventist history like a flow of historiography. It is a flow from missionary memory to Nigerian agency. The exploration of the flow of Adventist mission historiography in Nigeria will be demonstrated in three stages.

A. *Missio Dei, Motus Dei*, and Missionary-Centric Narratives (1900s–1940s)

These narratives were typically authored by missionaries themselves or their institutions. They emphasized geographical expansion, medical missions, and educational development, often through Eurocentric lenses. For example, the early missions in Southern Nigeria are depicted as "trailblazing" efforts, yet this book notes that West African missionaries were key to rooting Adventism, although largely unrecognized. Further exploration is given to the intricate and complex relationships of Seventh-day Adventist missionaries with indigenous issues during their mission work in Nigeria.

B. Institutional Expansion, Conflict, and Revivals (1940s–1990s)

With Nigerian independence and the civil war, Adventist missions encountered both opportunity and crisis. Yet these are often under-explored. For example, the devastation of the civil war for Southeastern Nigerian Adventists is only sparsely documented and requires further historiographic investigation. Here again, despite the challenges, the resilience of many who went through the civil war is depicted. They bounced back to rebuild their mission following the movement of God (*motus Dei*).

C. Critical and Indigenous Reclamation (1990s–Present)

Former attempts to write Adventist history from African perspectives often rely on oral histories, sociopolitical analysis, and theological critique. While this is not a complete historical account of Adventism in Nigeria, which has been attempted by some, albeit incomplete in several ways,[43] this book situates itself here as part of a historiographical shift that values "Nigerian Adventist agency," not just missionary vision.

Consequently, the second chapter proposes a critical turn in Adventist mission historiography, one that asks who the real pioneers of Adventist mission in Nigeria were. The third chapter explores the intricate relationships between official Adventist missionaries and their Christian counterparts with the colonial authorities. The fourth chapter investigates the approach of Adventist missionaries to indigenous culture. The fifth chapter deals with how Adventist mission thrived in the 1940s to the late 1980s, highlighting serious issues such as independence, civil war, and campus revivals. In the last chapter, the forward-looking theme of *Nkeiruka* plays a role in understanding how a unique Nigerian Adventism may emerge in the future.

---

43. Nigerian Adventists have attempted to document the history of Adventism in Nigeria. Most have taken time frame, thematic, or regional approaches to their narrative. Yet until now, there is no one definite attempt to document the history of Adventism in Nigeria. Nevertheless, what exists remains commendable. See Anosike, "Development"; Agboola, *Seventh-day Adventists in Yorubaland, 1914–1964*; Kuranga, "Seventh-day Adventism in Western Nigeria"; Maigadi, *Adventist Church in Northern Nigeria*; Alalade, *Limiting Factors*.

Chapter 2

The Beginnings
Trailblazers of Adventism in Western and Southern Nigeria, 1900s–1930s

THE PEW RESEARCH CENTER reports of 2011 showed that out of the 80 million (50.8 percent) Christians in Nigeria, there are 60 million Protestants (or broadly defined 37.8 percent), 20 million Catholics (11 percent), 40,000 Orthodox Christians, and 810,000 other Christians.[1] In 2015, Pew noted that Nigeria's Christian population had risen to 87 million.[2] Among Protestants, mainline, mission churches, Pentecostal, and/or Nigerian Initiated churches play key roles in the religious and social arena of Nigeria. Among the mission churches, Seventh-day Adventists with about 335,019 members[3] constitute a small percentage of Protestants in Nigeria. One of the reasons for this might be that they were latecomers to the religious scene of Nigeria.

---

1. Pew Research Centre's Forum on Religion and Public Life Global Christianity, "Global Christianity"; Pew Research Centre's Forum on Religion and Public Life Global Christianity, "Nigeria."
2. See Gramlich, "Fast Facts About Nigeria."
3. *2025 Annual Statistical Report*, 19, 20, 21.

While the earliest Christian mission to Nigeria can be traced back to sixteenth-century Catholic missionaries[4] and to the late 1840s for Protestant missionaries, Adventism only arrived in Nigeria in the early part of the twentieth century. This lateness of arrival is explored more in detail in the next chapter and reiterated in chapter 4.

Popular opinion and several historical monographs have placed the coming of Seventh-day Adventists to Nigeria in 1914. The account claims the American Adventist missionary, David C. Babcock, along with two other Africans, R. P. Dauphin and Samuel D. Morgue, as the first missionaries to Nigeria. According to this popular study, while Babcock and his team started work in Western Nigeria in 1914, Jesse Clifford, the British Adventist missionary, started work in Southeastern Nigeria in 1923, and John J. Hyde began mission work in Northern Nigeria in 1931.[5] Hence, Babcock (and his associates), Clifford, and Hyde are until today considered the pioneers of Adventism in Nigeria. This is the main reason why Babcock University was named after Babcock as the pioneer missionary in Nigeria. Following this tradition, when another Adventist university was founded in 2013 (approved by the government in 2016) in the Southeast of Nigeria, it was called Clifford University in honor of the pioneer work of Jesse Clifford in that region. However, while it is true that these missionaries labored to establish Adventism in different areas in Nigeria, historical data shows that before them, James Hyatt, as well as Sydney Hayford and Benjamin Tikili, had been working in Nigeria.

This chapter[6] seeks to highlight the contribution of unknown key pioneer Adventist missionaries in Nigeria to give credence to the work of those who have not been adequately recognized. The focus here is mostly on personalities and their approach(es) to

---

4. Isichei, *History of Christianity in Africa*, 45.

5. Anosike, "Development"; Agboola, *Seventh-day Adventists in Yorubaland, 1914–1964*; Kuranga, "Seventh-day Adventism in Western Nigeria"; Maigadi, *Adventist Church in Northern Nigeria*; Alalade, *Limiting Factors*; Eregare, *African Christian Church History*; Eregare, *Groundwork*.

6. Originally published as "Trailblazers of Adventism in Nigeria, 1900s–1930s," *Journal of Adventist Mission Studies* 15 (2020) 1–13.

mission. Here it is demonstrated that the pioneer work in Nigeria occurred in at least two phases: (1) commissioned laymen and self-supporting missionaries, and (2) ordained and commissioned missionaries. In addition, the chapter shows that West African missionaries were key to rooting Adventism in Nigeria.

PHASE 1: COMMISSIONED LAYMEN AND SELF-SUPPORTING MISSIONARIES

Laymen here will be termed as those who were not commissioned ministers but who were enlisted as licentiates and served as missionaries doing medical and teaching jobs. This was the case of James (who was not ordained) and Marian Hyatt.[7] Self-supporting missionaries are those who did some mission work in addition to their jobs as in the case of Sydney Hayford and Benjamin I. Tikili.

Western Nigeria Part 1: James Hyatt

James M. Hyatt was a Black American medical missionary who worked together with his wife Marian in Ghana, Sierra Leone, and Nigeria. Born in 1869 in Denver, Colorado, James Hyatt went on to become a dentist. He married Marian (a seamstress and dress maker) on December 21, 1892.[8] In 1902, he was to go to Nyasaland (Malawi) after the Foreign Mission Board sent a request on his behalf to the Colorado Conference.[9] Although this did not materialize, two years later, in March 1903, James and Marian Hyatt entered Ghana as the first official Afro-American Adventist missionaries in that country and in all of West Africa.[10] Later, in 1905, they went to Sierra Leone where James Hyatt worked briefly for a year as the first Adventist missionary,[11] followed by David C. Babcock.

   7. Foreign Mission Board, "Minutes" (1903), 92.
   8. Williams, *Precious Memories of Missionaries of Color* 2:40.
   9. Foreign Mission Board, "Minutes" (1902), 65.
   10. Owusu-Mensa, *Saturday God and Adventism in Ghana*, 67.
   11. *Seventh-day Adventist Yearbook 1906*, 86; Hyatt, "West Africa," 13.

Between 1906 and 1907, Hyatt went on to work in Nigeria. He must have been working from Lagos for that period since the 1907 *Yearbook of Seventh-day Adventists* lists his name under the ministerial directory as a licentiate working in Nigeria.[12] However, after 1907, he was no longer listed in the church records. In *Precious Memories of Missionaries of Color*, James Hyatt is reported to have returned to the United States where he continued itinerant preaching and colporteur work.[13]

However, it seems Hyatt left the ministry and began a private dentistry practice in Liberia and later in Ghana.[14] The General Conference (GC) committee minutes of 1910 notes that Hyatt, "a colored man, is not now associated with our work, and owing to family troubles, his wife left him."[15] Sadly, Hyatt had started paying indiscrete attention to another woman[16] and physically abused his wife. That year, his wife, Marian Hyatt, had desired to return to America because of her health. The GC committee voted thus: "That we request Elder D. C. Babcock to investigate the case of Mrs. Marion [sic] Hyatt, and authorize him to send her home if she so desires, or if he thinks it proper, to arrange for her to do missionary work in Liberia."[17] After some time, Marian Hyatt returned home to America where she stayed with her sister in Michigan. She died after a severe illness on January 21, 1917.[18]

Three years later, James Hyatt died in a tragic accident on July 14, 1920, killed by a truck (lorry) in Ghana.[19] In spite of these problems, James Hyatt was the first Adventist missionary to land in Nigeria. Since there is a scarcity of information relating to his work there, applying insights from his work in Ghana and Sierra

12.. *Seventh-day Adventist Yearbook 1907*, 101.

13. Williams, *Precious Memories of Missionaries of Color* 2:44.

14. Langford, Letter to E. E. Andross, August 23, 1920. Hyatt, "West Africa," 13.

15. General Conference Committee, "Minutes" (1910).

16. Serns, Letter to J. L. Shaw, October 3, 1920.

17. General Conference Committee, "Minutes" (1910).

18. Serns, Letter to J. L. Shaw, October 3, 1920.

19. Linnel, Letter to J. L. Shaw, June 9, 1921.

Leone may be helpful in our reflection. While he was in those countries, he held Bible studies,[20] carried out evangelistic meetings accompanied with a vibrant music ministry, taught classes at the mission school,[21] and did medical mission work as a dentist.[22]

If he did some of these activities in Nigeria, then the appeals from those whom he reached is evidence of his efforts. Such type of appeals, reported by David C. Babcock in 1909, were published in the *Advent Review and Sabbath Herald*: "The appeals that have been made from Northern and Southern Nigeria demand our immediate attention. Here permanent stations should be built up soon."[23] Babcock noted earlier in the report that "while speaking in public recently, a lady in the congregation arose, and made an earnest request for us to open our work in Lagos, the capital of Southern Nigeria. This lady is the wife of a leading physician in Lagos and is quite a talented woman."[24]

Southern Nigeria Part 1: Sydney Hayford and Benjamin I. Tikili

In the same report, Babcock notes, "One brother is now on the Benne River teaching school, another is teaching at Bonney, and at Lokoja our books are read with much interest."[25] The said brother teaching at Bonny was Sydney Hayford, the son of J. D. Hayford, a Ghanaian mining landowner who also did Adventist pioneer lay work in the Gold Coast.[26] Hayford would go "out at times into the streets in the early morning to tell people about the soon coming of Christ, the true Sabbath, etc."[27] He also trained young men to become Bible

---

20. Hyatt, "West Africa," 13.
21. Hyatt, "West Africa," 19.
22. Owusu-Mensa, *Saturday God and Adventism in Ghana*, 67.
23. Babcock, "Work in West Africa."
24. Babcock, "Work in West Africa," 16.
25. Babcock, "Work in West Africa," 16.
26. Owusu-Mensa, *Saturday God and Adventism in Ghana*, 65.
27. Hale, "Gold Coast, West Africa," 16.

teachers. His desire to reach people with the Adventist message was passed on to his son Sydney, who became a government schoolmaster for the British colonial administration in Nigeria. While Sydney Hayford worked for the colonial government, he began doing "some" Adventist mission work in Bonny, Southern Nigeria.

Sydney Hayford's efforts in Nigeria are known due to J. D. Hayford's letter to Dudley Hale. Hayford writes, "No doubt it will interest you also to learn that my youngest son, Sydney, now fully come to the age of manhood, and who has been at Bonny, in Southern Nigeria, as a government schoolmaster for one or two years, has been doing some earnest work as a Seventh-day Adventist. He is an earnest lad, that good boy of mine is, and I bless God for him."[28] Sydney was the one who introduced Benjamin I. Tikili (from Nembe, of the Brass people in Niger Delta) to Adventism.

Tikili, who was born into the home of practitioners of African (Nigerian) traditional religion, began learning of Christianity when he was sent to school in Bonny, Nigeria. He later became an ordained minister in 1924, working as a pioneer missionary under Jesse Clifford in the Niger Delta regions of Southern Nigeria and later in Ghana.

It is interesting how Tikili was introduced to Adventism. Around January 1919, when Tikili became a student in the Normal College or Teachers' Training Institute in Bonny, he began studying the Bible on his own. Then he became friends with Sydney Hayford, who taught him that the seventh day is the Sabbath and the biblical day of worship. Tikili began keeping the Sabbath but was ridiculed by his fellow students. Then he asked his teacher (Hayford) if there were people who kept the Sabbath. In response, he was given an address of Adventists in America. Tikili ordered two books through this address and continued studying Adventist beliefs. Tikili led two others to the same convictions he had come to. They joined his small "Adventist" band of indigenous Sabbath-keepers.

In 1921/22, when Tikili finished his studies at the Institute in Bonny, he was appointed as a teacher at Aba Government School.

28. Hale, "Gold Coast, West Africa," 16.

According to Tikili, he and two others remained Adventists until the official missionary (Jesse Clifford) was sent to Aba in 1923. It is possible that when L. F. Langford, William McClements, and Jesse Clifford toured Southeastern Nigeria, they met with the few Adventists of Tikili's group and other indigenous Sabbath-keeping groups. In Tikili's testimony, he claims, "My life in the Government school became a light, and many scholars started to make enquiries, which brought them to the faith."[29] This testimony is evident of Tikili's continual work as an indigenous "Adventist" mission worker in addition to his job as a teacher for the British colonial administration. Evidence for a small group of Adventists is found in a letter, possibly from Tikili, which was read by E. R. Palmer at the General Conference committee of April 16, 1923. The letter talks of a "number of new Sabbath-keepers in the Southern part" of Nigeria "who had taken their stand as a result of reading a copy of 'Present Truth' bearing a date in 1916."[30]

Sydney Hayford may have not been an ardent Adventist as his father claimed, for Tikili referred to him as "a partial Sabbath-keeper."[31] Nevertheless, Sydney led Tikili to the Adventist faith. Tikili in turn led a few others. Tikili was not only the first convert in Southeast Nigeria, he was also a pioneer worker. The work of Hayford and Tikili served as a springboard for the mission efforts of Clifford when he came to Aba in 1923. Likewise, it is apt to conclude that it was the pioneer missionary efforts of James Hyatt in the West of Nigeria which prepared the ground for the coming of David C. Babcock to Nigeria.

Additionally, it is apt to conclude that pioneer Adventist work in Nigeria was started by laypeople: the Hyatt family of African American background and Hayford and Tikili of West African background. Hyatt may have been commissioned to survey the West of Nigeria. Hayford seems to have been a lone Adventist in the South until Tikili, an indigene, came into the picture. The efforts of these men have until now remained largely unknown.

29. Tikili, "Experiences and Convictions," 12.
30. General Conference Committee, "Minutes" (1923), 327.
31. Tikili, "Experiences and Convictions," 12.

PHASE 2: ORDAINED AND COMMISSIONED MISSIONARIES

Commissioned ministers are understood as those who served as seasoned missionaries and had already served as former pastors in their home countries, for example, Babcock, Clifford, and Hyde. I will also include R. P. Dauphin, who was ordained as a minister, Samuel D. Morgue, a licentiate, and James J. Hamilton, who were experienced West African commissioned missionaries.

Western Nigeria Part 2: David C. Babcock, Rudolf P. Dauphin, Samuel D. Morgue, and James J. Hamilton

According to original documents, the Nigerian Mission was organized in December 1913[32] while David C. Babcock went to Nigeria in 1914. Born in New Hampshire, Ohio, on September 12, 1854, Babcock studied at Battle Creek College in Michigan. He would later work as a local pastor and president of the Virginia Conference (1897–1900). He first served as a mission director of the British Guiana Mission until 1905. During that time, he lost his wife Ann Davis in 1901. He remarried Mina Bradshaw, who accompanied him to West Africa.[33]

Babcock came to Nigeria after serving in Sierra Leone and mostly in Ghana from ca. 1905 to 1913. Until this time, the West African mission of Adventists focused its strength mostly on Sierra Leone and Ghana. The Nigerian Mission was officially organized towards the end of 1913 when a missionary conference was held in Freetown, Sierra Leone. This conference, convened by Ludwig Richard Conradi, president of the European Division, recommended that the West African Mission be divided into three regions: (1) Nigeria, (2) Gold Coast (Ghana), and (3) Sierra Leone and

---

32. General Conference Department of Education, *Story of Our Church*, 548; *Seventh-day Adventist Yearbook 1914*, 123.

33. Alao, *90 Years*, 19.

Liberia. David Babcock was asked to take charge of the Nigerian mission.[34]

Consequently, Babcock and his family arrived in Lagos in March 1914 together with three other African missionaries, Rudolf P. Dauphin of Sierra Lone, Samuel D. Morgue of Ghana,[35] and James J. Hamilton of Sierra Leone. More should be said on Hamilton at this point. Nigerian Adventist historians have until today maintained that Babcock came with two West African missionaries. Hamilton has always been left out of Babcock's crew, possibly because information on this missionary from Sierra Leone is not readily available. Interestingly, he was mentioned by William McClements as a member of the group of missionaries led by Babcock to Western Nigeria.[36]

The Babcock team moved to establish the Adventist message in Erunmu, Ibadan (capital of the western region), in Yorubaland. It has been noted that one of Babcock's associates (possibly Morgue) learned the Yoruba language. This aided evangelistic communication of the early mission in Western Nigeria. In addition, Samuel Oyeniyi, the son of the Baale (ruler) of Erunmu, who started keeping the Sabbath, became the evangelistic translator for the missionaries.[37] Oyeniyi not only spoke Yoruba and English, but he also spoke Hausa, which is widely spoken in the Northern region. Having him on the team facilitated the progress of the Adventist mission reaching out from Erunmu further inland to Sao and Ipoti-Ekiti where the first mission station was built. The mastery of the local Yoruba language enabled the opening of three village mission schools and resulted in the baptism of about seven converts at the end of 1914.[38]

Babcock was not only an evangelist. He was also an educator. One notable Adventist mission advance by this team of

---

34. Alalade, *Limiting Factors*, 50; Alao, *90 Years*, 19.

35. Babcock, "Trials and Victories," 24; Kern, "Study of Our African Mission," 14.

36. McClements, "Outlook in Nigeria," 1; Read, "Itinerating in Nigeria," 3.

37. Agboola, *Seventh-day Adventist History in West Africa*, 24, 25.

38. Agboola, *Seventh-day Adventist History in West Africa*, 24, 25.

missionaries was the establishment of a school in Sao (Shao), Ilorin, in 1915/16. The school served the three stations of Erunmu, Sao, and Ipoti-Ekiti, and expanded to become the first formal Adventist educational institution in Nigeria. This was where early national workers for the mission were trained. These workers were mostly trained as evangelists in addition to reading, writing, and arithmetic, as well as in entrepreneurial skills like bricklaying, furniture making, carpentry, etc.[39] Although Babcock served as its head, the running of the school was possible because of the language prowess of his team members, comprised of Morgue and especially Oyeniyi, who became a teacher in the school.[40] Still, the educational feat of these early missionaries is not surprising since the establishment of educational institutions in mission stations was a prime Adventist mission strategy. Moreover, other Christian missionaries also used education during the colonial era.

Although Babcock spearheaded the mission work during this phase, the success of this phase of the mission came mainly from his African associates: Morgue, who learned the local language, and Oyeniyi, an indigene of the community. This supports Andrew Walls' argument that "most Africans have always heard the gospel from Africans, and virtually all the great movements towards the Christian faith in Africa have been African led [sic]."[41]

Ill health forced the Babcock family to leave Nigeria in October 1917. Ernest Ashton, his assistant, became the interim director of the mission. Shortly after, due to his wife's illness, Ashton also left Nigeria.[42] He was succeeded by L. F. Langford and William McClements, respectively.

---

39. Agboola, *Seventh-day Adventist History in West Africa*, 26.
40. Neufeld, "Nigeria Mission," 181.
41. Walls, *Cross-Cultural Process in Christian History*, 45.
42. Andross, *Story of the Advent Message*, 269.

Southern Nigeria Part 2: Jesse Clifford

Adventism's progress in the West of Nigeria started at first with an evangelistic endeavor and was aided by educational institutions.[43] In the Southeast where Adventism had more success, camp meetings gave the mission its initial push under the leadership of Jesse Clifford. Clifford, an English missionary, had served in Sierra Leone and Ghana. He arrived with his wife, Winnie D. Clifford, at Aba, Nigeria, in 1923 and began promoting evangelistic activities with the use of tracts, lantern slides, as well as through camp meetings.

According to some oral accounts, in 1922, Clifford (who was still scouting the mission field of Nigeria) got introduced to Daniel Ogbonna Onyeodo, a school worker in Aba, by fellow school worker C. H. Dede. At that time, Clifford needed a local Igbo interpreter for his missionary work among the Ngwa people. Onyeodo helped assemble and lead a team of outstanding students from the government school to serve as Clifford's interpreters. This team served not just as interpreters but as primary evangelists. As a result, some initial converts were Josiah Evo, Robert Abaribe, Philip Onwere, Mr. Adaelu, A. J. Dike, and Mr. Dinneya.[44]

In 1924, after Clifford convinced Tikili to join the ministry, the latter resigned from his government service to become an official mission worker (Tikili had been baptized the year before). This gave Clifford's work a boost. The ordination of Tikili brought in an additional minister with responsibility to do official mission as well as with the ability to conduct baptisms for several converts responding to Adventism. Another boost came through an educational program. With Tikili as headmaster, Clifford officially started a boy's primary school at Aba in 1927. This primary school and an additional Bible school became the basis of Adventist educational work in the Southeast of Nigeria.

In his approach to mission, Clifford experimented with Bible classes where he taught prospects how to read the Bible. He also

---

43. Nyekwere, *Medical Institutions*, 5.
44. Thankfully, this has been documented. See Anonaba, "Onyeodo."

THE BEGINNINGS

experimented with public evangelistic meetings. Nevertheless, the camp meetings held in 1928 and 1929 gave Adventism its initial success in Igboland.[45] It became an effective approach for missions in the Southeast. Aside from the fact that the Igbos were generally open to Christianity, one reason for this was that the camp meeting booth style, made of palm fronds, was suitable to the Ngwa Igbos who did not live in towns or cities but in compounds[46] with several thatch houses around. Other approaches used by Clifford included maintaining contacts with indigenous Sabbath-keepers,[47] writing a book in the Igbo language,[48] and opening an informal school.

Another approach used by the Clifford-led group was to regularly visit government schools and offices. Those visits proved successful as some students like C. H. Dede, Josiah Evoh, Philip Onwere, Daniel Onyeodor, and Robert Abaribe became Adventists and helped out in the newly established Adventist school. They all later became leaders of Adventism in that region. That same year, 1930, L. Edmond, who later replaced Clifford as the director of the Southeast Mission, opened another station in the Southeast in Elele. The Southeast continued to have the influence and direct contribution of Tikili until towards the end of the 1930s when he left Adventism and pulled others with him.

What led to the unfortunate disassociation of Tikili from the Adventist Church? In 1938, the global Adventist Sabbath School featured the outpouring of the Holy Spirit at Pentecost for its first-quarter study guide.[49] During this time, the membership of the growing church in Aba believed in the imminent manifestation of "the latter rain," the end-time Pentecostal outpouring of the Holy Spirit. By July and August, a kind of "spirit movement" began. This charismatic movement saw several members claiming the power

---

45. McClements, "Our First Camp-Meeting in Nigeria," 6.

46. Read, "Itinerating in Southern Nigeria," 18, 19; Clifford, "Southeast Nigeria," 9.

47. Clifford, "Into South Nigeria, West Africa," 13; McClements, "Itinerating in Nigeria," 12.

48. McClements, "Nigerian Union Mission," 2.

49. Izima, *Brief History*, 23, 24.

of the Spirit to see visions and dreams, heal the sick, raise the dead, make the lame to walk, etc. While some prophesied and spoke in tongues, others openly confessed their sins and were flogged publicly to gain forgiveness.[50]

The movement brought about two conflicting opinions. While some saw those manifestations as satanic counterfeits, another group, most probably led by Tikili, the indigenous and influential pastor, believed in the authenticity of the movement. When C. A. Bartlett attended the workers' meeting in August, his lecture on "Try the Spirits Whether They Are of God" seemed to diminish or quell the movement's momentum. With less support from the church leadership on this matter, Tikili resigned and established his own church (Seventh-day Church of God), taking with him some followers.[51]

The resignation of Tikili should not be a surprise considering his African traditional background. He must have seen the manifestation of the Spirit as part of indigenizing or localizing Adventism and making it culturally relevant. However, the mission leaders, who encouraged rationalism and order in worship, did not share his vision. This disagreement led to a schism, which possibly could have been avoided. Yet, this episode in history did not impede the success or growth of Adventism in the Southeast regions. The post-1930s historical growth attests to that fact. More of this is explored in chapter 4.

Northern Nigeria: John J. Hyde

Considering the success of the work in the Southeast and in the West, and with prospects also in the North, Nigeria was organized into three missions in 1930. The following year, 1931, as Clifford left to take charge of the mission in Ghana, John. J. Hyde, who had worked in Sierra Leone and Ghana, started mission work in Jengre, near Jos in Northern Nigeria. Before moving to Jengre, he resided

---

50. Izima, *Brief History*, 23, 24.
51. Izima, *Brief History*, 24; interview with Solomon O. Agharaumuna, 2019.

at Ibadan from where he made a survey for an appropriate station for the work in the North of Nigeria.[52] After Jengre was chosen as a mission station, Hyde moved there with his wife, Louisa Hyde, who was a trained nurse, and their son.

The Jengre area was mostly dominated by Muslims, which made mission work difficult. Therefore, the Hydes began a dispensary to use Mrs. Hyde's skills. The dispensary, which later became the Jengre SDA hospital, provided an avenue to reach the people around the Jengre area who were in dire need of medical treatment. One episode was the treatment of the jigger flea by Louisa Hyde. She extracted the parasite from the feet of those who came for medical assistance. This in turn captured the attention of the people around. In 1933, E. D. Dick, the secretary of the then Northern European Division (the parent Division from which the mission in Nigeria was organized), reported:

> The medical work under the direction of Sister Hyde, a trained nurse, is warming the hearts of the people. From twenty to thirty come for treatments and medicine each day. Some of these come from a distance of fifty miles or more. The spiritual side of the work is kept foremost, so that the patients can understand that it is God who brings relief from their distresses. The Sabbath services are attended by some forty to fifty each week, and a definite interest is manifested. Some who have been cured, refuse to return to their houses, as they wish to stay near the mission so they can attend the morning and Sabbath meetings.[53]

Once, when William McClements, superintendent of the mission in Nigeria, visited the Hydes, a delegation of about fifty chiefs came to inquire about the Adventist medical work. The men who were practicing traditionalists and cannibals expressed a need for Adventism in their area.[54] This inquiry led to a plan to conduct strong medical and evangelistic work among them. Although the

---

52. Maigadi, *Adventist Church in Northern Nigeria*, 38.
53. Dick, "West Coast of Africa," 10.
54. McClements, "Nigeria," 12.

plan did not materialize immediately, through the medical work in the North, some people easily responded to the Advent message even after initial resistance.[55]

In addition, Hyde understood the need to have a knowledge of the Hausa and Amo languages. He labored to build relationships in his community. A notable friendship was the relationship he had with the Kakwi family. The four sons of Kakwi—Lamba, Mayang, Filibus, and Simon— became his "disciples" and worked as pioneers in their community. They all later became Adventist workers.[56] Before John J. Hyde left for Sierra Leone in 1942, the work in the North of Nigeria had already gained some footholds: there had been baptisms[57] combined with the beginning of a semi-formal school where adult education was conducted.[58] Hyde was replaced by L. W. Normington and thus ended this phase of the Adventist mission enterprise in Nigeria. I will explore this phase again in the next chapter from the perspective of Adventism's beginnings in the North of Nigeria.

SUMMARY AND CONCLUSION

The beginnings of Adventism in Nigeria had a dynamic outlook. Pioneer mission work was done in different regions almost simultaneously. Hence, it is not possible to attribute the pioneer mission work to one or two persons. Rather, Nigeria had several pioneer Advent missionaries who came to Nigeria in phases. The work of these pioneers requires adequate documentation. James Hyatt, who was the first Black American missionary in West Africa, did pioneering mission work for Adventism in Nigeria and the groundwork he laid cannot be downplayed. While the work of Hyatt, Sydney Hayford, and Benjamin Tikili remains under research, the person and work of James J. Hamilton, Babcock's associate from

---

55. Maigadi, *Adventist Church*, 38, 39, 44.
56. Maigadi, *Adventist Church*, 44.
57. Hyde, "Progress in Northern Nigeria," 4.
58. Maigadi, *Adventist Church*, 44.

Sierra Leone, needs substantial historical treatment. Moreover, the work of indigenous African missionaries like Hayford, Tikili, and Oyeniyi who only receive one or two sentences in historical accounts has been vastly underestimated. It was the indigenous efforts of the early African leaders that contributed to the success of the mission in their regions.

Furthermore, the mission history of Adventism in the Southeast of Nigeria begs the following question: Where and when does the mission history of the denomination begin in an area or region? Does the history of a denomination begin when missionary X arrives in a region, sets up camp, builds a school and a church? Or does it begin with the acts of God (*missio Dei*), leading a particular people slowly and gradually to his gospel? As patterned in the conversion of Tikili, with a heritage of African traditional religion, the history of Adventist mission among the Igbos was a fluid and dynamic process where the acts of God laid the foundation for the establishment of Adventism in that region. This vision of a *missio Dei* hermeneutic, as outlined in chapter 1, is helpful in doing and writing mission history.

Chapter 3

Colonial Politics, Missionary Rivalry, and the Beginnings of Adventist Mission in Northern Nigeria

WHEN COMPARED TO ITS relative success in the Southern and Western parts of Nigeria, Adventism had some difficulties in establishing its mission in the North from the 1930s onward. This third chapter[1] argues that there were three reasons why Adventist missionaries found the North difficult. First, Adventist workers joined the Christian missionary scene in Nigeria rather late. Second, due to colonial politics, which did not favor the proselytizing aims of Christian missionaries in the North, Adventist missionaries did not find it easy to immediately establish a mission. Third, the difficult beginnings in Northern Nigeria can also be attributed to the relationship between Adventist missionaries and other mission bodies which tended towards rivalry because of the "spheres of influence" established by the colonial government.

1. Adapted from Nengel and Wogu, "Colonial Politics, Missionary Rivalry."

ADVENTISM IN NIGERIA, 1900-30

As was demonstrated in the previous chapter, the coming of Adventism to Nigeria was in two phases. The first phase comprised the mission attempts of commissioned laymen and self-supporting missionaries like James M. Hyatt, a Black lay missionary from the United States. Hyatt had been working in Ghana and Sierra Leone and went to Nigeria between 1906 and 1907. Another indigenous layman, Benjamin I. Tikili, contributed to the growth of a group of a few Adventists until Jesse C. Clifford was sent to Aba in 1923.

The second phase of the Adventist mission started around 1913 with ordained and commissioned missionaries who built upon the work of the first phase. This phase brought David C. Babcock together with three other West African workers: R. P. Dauphin, Samuel D. Morgue, and James J. Hamilton. As earlier stated in the previous chapter, Babcock seemed the most qualified to lead the mission. He had served as director of the British Guiana Mission until 1905 and came to Nigeria after serving in Sierra Leone and Ghana (approximately 1905-13). After the Nigerian mission was officially organized in 1913, the Babcock team arrived in 1914, focusing attention on Western Nigeria while based in Ibadan. In 1923, Southern Nigeria got its official missionary, Jesse C. Clifford, who got in touch with Tikili in Aba, from where Adventism spread in the South.[2]

Adventism in Southern Nigeria proved to be a more successful venture than in the West. The combined growth of both regions catalyzed a decision to officially reorganize the work, and the field became known as the Nigerian Union Mission with four constituent missions: Northeastern Nigerian Mission, Northwestern Nigerian Mission, Southeastern Nigerian Mission, and Southwestern Nigerian Mission.[3] There were two reasons for making such a decision, knowing that the Nigerian mission was largely among the

---

2. Wogu, "Trailblazers of Adventism in Nigeria."

3. Christian, "Annual Division Meeting," 2; McClements, "Nigerian Union Mission," 2; *Seventh-day Adventist Yearbook 1932*, 199-220.

Yorubas in the West and the Igbos in the Southeast, and without prospects in the North.

Firstly, William McClements, the leader of the Adventist work in Nigeria, was a visionary. Being aware that growth was strongest in the West,[4] he must have been enthusiastic to establish Adventism in the Muslim regions of the North. Around 1924, McClements baptized several converts in Ilorin and surrounding towns, although the area had a good number of Islamic adherents.[5] In 1930, McClements reported the opposition Adventism had experienced in and around Sosoki village in Ilorin Province (also known today as Yowere, in Kwara State). The opposition was settled after the local emir gave the Adventists some land on which to build a church.[6] Consequently, McClements must have thought it would be possible to establish a mission in the North.

Secondly, after Adventists had recorded a handful of successes in the face of opposition, plans were made for the North of Nigeria, starting with Ilorin. Although Ilorin was close to the Mission headquarters in Ibadan, the town was considered closer to the North because of its Muslim inhabitants. Hence, a mission station was established at Awtun in the Ilorin Province, probably as a base to fully enter the North.[7] This must have been the reason for making John J. Hyde the superintendent of the Northeast Mission.

Accordingly, in 1930, Hyde arrived in Nigeria with the intention of doing mission work in the North. However, things did not turn out as planned. It was not until 1932 that Hyde was firmly established and able to fully launch out from Jengre into several other Northern towns. Why did the establishment of a mission station in the North take so much time? Considering the data from extant sources mentioned below, the Adventist missionaries had difficulties in their attempts to establish a mission in Northern Nigeria for three reasons. Firstly, Adventists were latecomers to the Christian missionary scene in Nigeria. Secondly, the colonial

---

4. Ising, "Visiting West Africa," 4.
5. Lashier, "From West Africa," 3.
6. McClements, "Nigerian Union Mission," 2.
7. Ising, "Visiting West Africa," 4; Read, "Message in Nigeria," 14.

politics at that time did not favor the proselytizing aims of missionaries in the North. Finally, due to the "spheres of influence" established by colonial authorities, there was rivalry between the Adventist missionaries and the Sudan Inland Mission (SIM) workers, which slowed the Adventists' pace considerably.

Before expatiating on these points, a caveat on sources and viewpoint is helpful. To be able to tell the Adventist story in Northern Nigeria, a number of primary sources were consulted. The archival sources used to reconstruct the history were mostly found in the Nigerian national archives of Jos, Kaduna, and Zaria, especially letters and documents related to the establishment of the Adventist mission. While data dealing primarily with Muslim sources was not the focus here, some materials were consulted due to their relevance to the subject. Additionally, archival documents stored abroad were not consulted because of distance and data saturation found in Nigeria.

Furthermore, news items and mission reports of Adventist missionaries contained in extant Adventist periodicals added to the archival data found in Nigeria. Additionally, a number of historical works and monographs were consulted as supplements, especially in the article sections where I could only rely on published articles or books to augment archival sources.

ADVENTIST MISSIONARIES IN NIGERIA: LATECOMERS

Adventism was a latecomer to the missionary scene of Nigeria. Historically, there were two attempts to establish Christianity in Nigeria. The first dates back as far as the sixteenth century with Portuguese Catholic missionaries sent to the Kingdom of Benin.[8] However, the kingdom was in the middle of intertribal wars and was only interested in the religion if the missionaries came with a trade bag of firearms. Unable to make an impact, the missionaries

---

8. Egharevba, *History of Benin*, 26–27.

soon left.⁹ Some Catholic influence continued until the early 1800s, but not without interruption. Regrettably, the new religion remained confined to the royal court.¹⁰

Christian missionaries in Nigeria were more successful in their second attempt from around 1841 to 1914, when Protestant missionaries came from Britain with the aim of Christianizing the African continent. Of interest here is the exploration of the Niger River (1830–57), which was "intended to undermine the slave trade . . . and to open up the Africa interior to Christianity and commerce."¹¹ It laid the foundation for the Christianization of cities along the Niger and in Igboland through the Niger expedition. The expeditions had freed slaves and educated Christians as members, including Samuel Ajayi Crowther, who later became the first African Anglican bishop.

With the opening of Yorubaland (West and Southwest), Igboland (South/Southeast), and the Hausa regions (North) by the CMS, other Christian missions followed suit, so that by the turn of the twentieth century several Christian churches had gained a footing in Nigeria. Moreover, as Christianity was spreading rapidly in the South, Islam, through its jihad conquests, was spreading in the Northern region and to the South, invading Oyo and Ilorin until it was defeated in Oshogbo by the Ibadan army.

Furthermore, by the early twentieth century, British colonial rule, which had begun in the nineteenth century, established a firm grasp on present-day Nigeria. The modern Nigerian state originated when the Southern and Northern Protectorates were amalgamated by Lord Frederick Lugard in 1914. It was the same year that Adventists officially entered the West of Nigeria through David Babcock and his African missionary associates after unsuccessful earlier attempts.

Therefore, by the time Adventists arrived, the Nigerian missionary arena was marked by significant missionary presence in

---

9. Ajayi, *Christian Missions*, 2; Watson, "Benin City Nigeria," 126.

10. Baur, *2000 Years of Christianity in Africa*, 76; Hastings, *Church in Africa, 1450–1950*, 119; Ajayi, *Christian Missions*, 3.

11. Isichei, *History of Christianity in Africa*, 171.

the West and South, and in Islamic strongholds in the North, all governed by colonial governmental policies. As latecomers, Adventists had to deal with these elements. In the West and especially the South, Adventism was successful. The North, with different colonial policies and an Islamic presence, was not entered until the 1930s, and its colonial policy regarding Christian proselytizing caused some difficulty for Adventists.

CHRISTIAN MISSION AND REGIONAL AUTHORITIES: COLONIAL POLITICS AND THE IMPLEMENTATION OF INDIRECT RULE

The colonization of Nigeria was a prolonged process. According to Falola and Heaton, it took more than forty years because "circumstances and the influence of missionaries, traders or French and German incursions tended to dictate the process of colonization; in the end however, territories were brought into submission only by the use of force."[12] The use of force helped to unify independent states, regions, and kingdoms. In the case of Nigeria, Falola and Heaton have argued that colonization "brought under the sole rule of the United Kingdom previously independent states that had been interconnected commercially and to some extent culturally over the previous centuries but had not experienced political unification of any kind."[13] Hence modern Nigeria was birthed by unifying several kingdoms, chieftaincies, and independent states belonging to the Southern and Northern Protectorates.

However, colonial rule in Nigeria did not stop at mere unification. Indirect rule was used by the British to control and supervise colonies through preexisting indigenous power structures. In Nigeria, while indirect rule was not successful in the South, it functioned well in the northern regions. The colonial administration in Northern Nigeria had significant policies governing the opening of the Christian missions and operations in the region.

12. Falola and Heaton, *History of Nigeria*, 109.
13. Falola and Heaton, *History of Nigeria*, 109.

When Lugard conquered the Sokoto Caliphate between 1900 and 1905, being quite aware of Islamic sensibilities, he promised the Muslim rulers that he was not going to interfere with their religion. This promise, as Andrews Barnes has established, was made under the false assumption that Islam was by default the religion of the people in the North.[14] The implication of this was that Christian missionaries were permitted to propagate their religion only among non-Muslim societies. There were two reasons for this.

Firstly, by this time, Christianity was quite successful among non-Muslim societies. Factors such as the introduction of educational programs, the use of medical work, and the influence of Black/African missionaries contributed to the success.[15] These positive developments caused Muslims to resent Christian missionaries and their converts. According to Marinus C. Iwuchukwu, contrary to Islamic theological teachings, Christians were generally considered as unbelievers—*kafir*—by the Fulani Muslims north of the Niger.[16] This hatred was also transferred to the British colonial authorities, seen as agents of Christian propagation. Therefore, to show that their presence in the Hausa and Fulani territories had nothing to do with the Christians, or with being seen as advocates of Christianity, Lugard and his associates had to emphasize their position by promising not to interfere with the Islamic religion. This eventually earned Lugard the loyalty and cooperation of the northern leaders and the promotion of indirect rule.[17]

Secondly, it is possible that Lugard himself had come to dislike educated Christian converts who mostly came from the South. In fact, it seems he saw them as threats to successful indirect rule. Therefore, he "disdained the European-educated Nigerians . . . claiming that mission schools inculcated in their pupils 'discontent [sic] impatience of any control, and an unjustifiable assumption of self-importance in the individual,' all of which

14. Barnes, "'Evangelization.'"
15. Danmole, "Religion and Politics"; Faught, "Missionaries, Indirect Rule"; Galadima and Turaki, "Christianity in Nigeria."
16. Iwuchukwu, *Muslim-Christian Dialogue*, 22.
17. Iwuchukwu, *Muslim-Christian Dialogue*, 20, 21.

made the educated Nigerians a threat to both the British rule and traditional social norms."[18]

Lugard not only disliked the Christian converts but also had a certain level of distrust toward missionaries because they empowered the converts. Thus, he encouraged every colonial administrator to "cordially welcome the establishment of Missions among pagan tribes—except, perhaps, that type of mission . . . whose actions however well intentioned, degrade the European in the eyes of the native."[19] Put differently, Lugard did not want any Christian ideology of empowerment that would interfere with indirect rule or challenge colonial powers in the Muslim North. In fact, as he made clear in his "Amalgamation Report," the colonial authorities wanted "to ensure that a class of Christian converts did not arise to challenge British authority in the North as they had in the South."[20]

Nevertheless, Iwuchukwu, likely through the influence of E. O. Ayandele, argues that Lugard was not completely opposed to Christian missionaries and their activities but just ensured that they did not tarnish the relationship with the Northern leaders nor hurt his administration there.[21] This argument holds, for despite the restrictions, Lugard made some exceptions to the CMS missionaries, since his mother was a missionary in the same organization. Besides, he regarded CMS missionaries as educated men "with sympathies similar to those of colonial officials."[22] Additionally, aside from his friendship with Walter Miller, a CMS missionary, during Lugard's leadership, permission was given to some Christian mission endeavors in parts of the North: the Toronto Industrial Mission at Pategi (1899); CMS in Bida (1902) and Zaria City (1904); the Cambridge University Mission Party (later Sudan United Mission, SUM) in Wase, Nassarawa Province; and the Mennonite Brethren of the USA in Ilorin (1905).[23]

18. Falola and Heaton, *History of Nigeria*, 129.
19. Lugard, *Dual Mandate*, cited in Barnes, "'Evangelization,'" 427.
20. Barnes, "'Evangelization,'" 428.
21. Iwuchukwu, *Muslim-Christian Dialogue*, 23.
22. Barnes, "'Evangelization,'" 424.
23. Iwuchukwu, *Muslim-Christian Dialogue*, 24.

However, in 1906 when Lugard resigned as high commissioner of Northern Protectorate, the restrictions placed on Christian mission activities in the North tightened. Iwuchukwu has explored the relationship between Christian missions and colonial authorities. Emmanuel M. Abar has argued that this relationship of power politics was not only between representatives of the Christian mission and colonial authorities but also incorporated other parties: members of the Islamic religion and practitioners of traditional religions.[24] Iwuchukwu demonstrates that during the administrations of Percy Girouard and Sir Hasketh Bell, Lugard's successors, "restrictions of Christian mission activities was [sic] even more severe and the application of the Indirect Rule system arrogated more powers to the emirs and less interference by the colonial administrators."[25]

Iwuchukwu further notes that in these periods "Christians were not only restricted from Muslim areas but also denied access to the non-Muslim minority ethnicities."[26] The restrictions were severe, to the extent that Bell's assistant, Charles L. Towers, was well known for considering Christian missionaries as the "greatest menace" in the scheme of the British administration in the North. At the same time, the chiefs of Kabwir (Kano) and Sura were deposed for their active interest in Christianity.[27]

With such restrictions, Christian missionaries did not remain silent. They began petitioning the local colonial authorities. In a 1911 letter written by the SIM, a resident officer was accused of tearing down churches, being motivated to promote Islam: "It has come to the knowledge of your Memorialists that some of the Resident Administrators in Northern Nigeria are of the opinion that it is the purpose and policy of your Government to allow free course to the propagation of the Mohammedan religion amongst

---

24. Abar, "Islam, Christianity, Traditional Religions."
25. Iwuchukwu, *Muslim-Christian Dialogue*, 25.
26. Iwuchukwu, *Muslim-Christian Dialogue*, 25.
27. Iwuchukwu, *Muslim-Christian Dialogue*, 26.

Pagan tribes, while ... Missionaries of the Cross should be permitted to work only under a special privilege and license."[28]

H. J. Read, from the office of the Under Secretary of the State for Colonies, responded and requested missionaries disentangle themselves from local affairs: "There will be a tendency among converts to pay more attention to the advice of the white missionary than to the orders of their own Ruler, and it is to be hoped that those who are engaged in mission work detach themselves, as much as possible, from interference in local secular affairs."[29]

The missionaries changed their tactics, accusing the colonial government of obstructing religious liberty. This seemed to have rattled the authorities' resolve. They rallied together and responded that "the restrictions then in effect on Christian proselytizing in the North were 'not contrary to the principles of religious toleration.'"[30] Yet, the colonial authorities were afraid that missionaries would use their race as a battering ram to subdue and break down the emirs' authority. Hence, according to E. J. Arnett, an officer in Sokoto, to let Christian missionaries work among Muslims was not a question of toleration "but of teaching Christianity at the point of a bayonet."[31] This was necessary, since some colonial administrators thought the Protestant missionaries' main aim was an increase of converts. In addition, there were Black missionaries like W. A. Thompson, a Caribbean CMS worker, who taught that all men are equal.[32] Such ideas annoyed colonial authorities. Thus, colonial officers not only disliked White missionaries for their

---

28. National Archives of Kaduna, (NAK) SNP 7, 3754/1911 (1930, 1931, 1932), files and letters related to Christian Missions/Establishment of Seventh-day Adventist Mission, cited in Barnes, "'Evangelization,'" 428.

29. Cited in Barnes, "'Evangelization,'" 429; N.A.K. SNP 7, 3754/1911.

30. Cited in Barnes, "'Evangelization,'" 429.

31. Arewa House Archives (A.H.A.), Kaduna, 15246, cited in Barnes, "'Evangelization,'" 429.

32. Barnes, "'Evangelization,'" 421, 422. W. A. Thompson spent over thirty years in Nigeria where he worked on the translation of the Bible and the Prayer Book into the Nupe and Hausa languages. See Newmann, "Caribbean's Response," 21.

efforts, but they also totally disdained those Black missionaries who undermined their authority and racial ideologies.

Furthermore, around 1917, the various Protestant missions in the North banded together to exert pressure on the colonial government. This time, the missionaries "changed their line of attack from accusing administrators of favoritism toward Islam to insisting that in Northern Nigeria the Colonial Office follow the same principle of religious toleration [as] in the rest of the empire."[33] Although Sir Hugh Clifford, who by 1924 was the governor of Nigeria, insisted that the entry of Christian missions into the Muslim territories might arouse religious fanaticism, the argument of religious tolerance sounded very reasonable to Sir Graeme Thomson, appointed governor in 1927. One of his first acts was a promise to relax the restrictions. He also gave a mandate to colonial administrators to help missionaries "identify possible sites in Muslim territories for mission stations."[34]

However, Thomson's mandate was resisted to some extent by his subordinates. For instance, in 1928, the CMS was expelled from Zaria City, a decision highly influenced by H. R. Palmer, the lieutenant-governor and an advocate for exclusion of Christians from the North.[35] In addition, H. Herman-Hodge, the resident in Ilorin, even argued that the government had granted "too much latitude" to the missionaries and "placed much reliance in their good faith."[36] Therefore, in the face of this resistance it is not surprising that at the Miango Conference (near Jos) in 1929, the mission societies interested in carrying out their activities in the North "expressed utter disgust with the policy of excluding the missionaries" from Muslim regions.[37] As a result, it was agreed the matter would be discussed in a meeting at London with the governor of Nigeria.[38]

33. Barnes, "'Evangelization,'" 414.
34. Barnes, "'Evangelization,'" 414.
35. Ubah, "Christian Missionary."
36. Cited in Barnes, "'Evangelization,'" 431.
37. Ubah, "Christian Missionary," 17.
38. Ubah, "Christian Missionary," 17.

Consequently, in London, 1930, Dr. Oldham, secretary of International Missionary Council or International Council of Missions, arranged a meeting of the heads of Missions, government officials, and the governor of Nigeria. A consensus was reached since the governor seemingly allowed mission access to the emirates of Northern Nigeria. Nonetheless, the colonial government was not interested in applying "pressure on the emirs with a view to making them allow the missionaries into their territories."[39] On the other hand, Ubah relates, the authorities promised not to do anything "which might give the emirs the impression that it expected them to reject requests for missionary enterprise. The government was interested in educating the emirs on the principles of religious toleration but would do so gradually."[40]

At this point, although there was no clarity in the relaxation of the restrictions, the 1930s began with renewed hope for missionizing the Muslim North. Palmer, who had been serving as lieutenant-governor, was replaced in 1930 by C. W. Alexander, who "was not committed to the preservation of the status quo in the North."[41] Thus, a letter from the new lieutenant-governor's office requested the colonial resident officers give a complete report on the missionary progress in the Muslim areas of the province.[42] In the administrators' replies, the spirit of resistance still colored the reports, which either undermined the missionaries' deficiencies or lack of success. Yet, the fact that there were some positive notes showed that things were changing for the better.[43]

In 1931, when Sir Donald Cameron replaced Thomson as governor of Nigeria, the "coming of a new governor may have suggested to the missionaries that this was a good opportunity to try again before he fell into the hands of the anti-missionary groups."[44]

39. Ubah, "Christian Missionary," 17.
40. Ubah, "Christian Missionary," 17.
41. Ubah, "Christian Missionary," 18.
42. Arewa House Archives (A.H.A.), 5533, vol. 1, 188, as quoted in Barnes, "'Evangelization,'" 430.
43. Barnes, "'Evangelization,'" 432–33.
44. Ubah, "Christian Missionary," 18.

That year, during his first visit to Kaduna—the headquarters of the Northern Provinces administration—Cameron held an important conference with representatives of the SIM, the SUM, and the CMS. At the meeting, H. G. Farrant (SUM) "made the point that it was four years since Sir Graeme Thomson promised a change of policy, and the missions wished to know what the chances were of their being allowed to acquire sites for the purpose of missionary and other activities."[45] Cameron's response may be summarized as follows: Missionary efforts could proceed cautiously and with the right personnel; there was to be no interference with administration; missions were to operate within distinct spheres of influence (which was not a new idea); and a prohibition on public preaching in the emirates was readily accepted by the missionaries.[46]

With the official policy, those areas and regions earlier dominated by mission societies were agreed upon as their spheres of influence. The Roman Catholic Mission (RCM) and the CMS had carved out their spheres around Lokoja and Nupeland and parts of Benue Province, including Shendam, which initially was administered as part of Muri Province. The SIM and SUM dominated most parts of Niger Province, Southern Zaria, and Plateau Provinces, including Kaltungo in Gombe and Mubi in Southern Borno Province, while the Lutheran Church had its headquarters at Numan in Adamawa Province.[47]

Therefore, as the policy of restriction was being relaxed, there was a developing relationship between the colonial administration and some Christian missions. At the same time, the Christian missions in the North seemed to have settled internal squabbles and became more organized, with a united goal of missionizing the North. Barnes concludes that it was because of their previous struggle with the administrators that they were able to fully work a division of territories based on the concept of "spheres of

---

45. Ubah, "Christian Missionary," 18.

46. Ubah, "Christian Missionary," 18–19.

47. Crampton, *Christianity in Northern Nigeria*; Kalu, *Christianity in West Africa*.

influence."[48] During that time, the Adventists arrived, oblivious to the *zeitgeist* that ruled the colonial Muslim North.

ADVENTIST MISSIONARIES AND OTHER CHRISTIAN MISSIONS IN NIGERIA: MISSION RIVALRY

When the Adventists appeared on the scene after three decades of the imposition of colonial rule in the North, almost all the available spheres of influence had been allocated to the earlier missionaries. The spheres of influence became the source of rivalry between Adventists and the SIM, explored below.

A Reconnoitering Visit

With the aim of carrying out mission activities across the northern banks of the Rivers Niger and Benue, three Adventist leaders visited Jos to explore the possibility of entering Plateau Province. The team consisted of McClements, superintendent of the Adventist Mission in Nigeria, W. E. Read, president of the West African Mission fields, and John J. Hyde, director of Northeast Mission. On arrival, they were granted audience with the resident of Plateau Province on February 9, 1931. During the interview, the purpose of the visit was succinctly spelled out: "They wished to open a Medical Mission in the Plateau Province." In response, the resident "gave a brief resume of the position of Missions in the Plateau Province ... [and] suggested that the [Adventist] Mission should get in touch with the Council of Missions and put up concrete proposals, when the matter could be further considered."[49]

It is likely that the "Council of Missions" was the International Council of Missions or International Missionary Council which was constituted in 1921 and integrated into the World Council of Churches in 1961. The Council was in England, where

48. Barnes, "'Evangelization,'" 436.
49. Clarke and Monsell, "Spheres of Influence of Missionary Societies."

its secretary, Dr. Oldham, had organized the stakeholders' meeting of 1930 regarding mission access to the emirates. Thus, the Council had become an important player in advising the colonial office on this matter. Until this time, Adventists were either very hesitant to ecumenical endeavors or maintained a very low involvement with other mission bodies.[50] Thus, they had little or no dealings with the Council. Hence, they did not consult other Christian missionaries on this matter and were not informed of the politics in place. In any case, the team was asked to formally request a sphere of influence for its operation, which was possible after consulting with the Council.

Without reference to the Council of Missions, Hyde submitted a formal application for the establishment of an Adventist mission station in Plateau Province. On February 12, 1931, a telegram was sent from Kaduna to the resident of Plateau Province, who in turn directed it to the officer in charge of Pankshin Division: "[Adventist] Mission whose work at present [is] confined to the Southern Provinces [is] anxious to open a Station in Northern Provinces. Essential site should be in or near country [with] high altitude but not clashing with sphere of any other Mission. [The] Station will combine (a) Leper Work (b) Native Hospital (c) Health Station for European Missionaries. Indicate by telegram what localities you suggest as suitable. Proposal is for single Station and not wide sphere of influence."[51]

Although there was no consultation with other missionaries, during the interview with the resident of Plateau Province, Hyde must have gotten an inclination that the colonial administrators preferred mission activities that helped to alleviate social and economic problems, which may explain their starting with medical missions in the North. As Shobana Shankar observes, the colonial administrators were fearful of "propaganda." Hence, they "recommended that medical missions first be let into 'pagan' areas of Northern Nigeria, where they could prove their trustworthiness to

---

50. Editorial, "Our Relationship to Other Societies"; Höschele, "Interchurch Relations."

51. N.A.K. Zar. Prof. 41, 1932.

native and British authorities and then later be rewarded with sites in Muslim areas."[52]

Doing medical missions on the peripheries of Muslim-dominated regions was in line with Cameron's policy of establishing work on the fringes which gave allowance to be invited by the emirs. It was also in line with Lugard's program of social reform, which he hoped Christians would carry out.[53]

After due consideration of the Adventist application, on February 23, 1931, the resident of Plateau Province conveyed the response of the divisional officer in charge of Pankshin: "There is no area on the high ground of Pankshin suitable for the establishment of a new Mission, as the [SUM] is already operating in the Gindiri, Sura, and Hill Angas Districts and has sent evangelists to the Kaleri and Ron Districts."[54]

On the advice of the Plateau resident, two alternative locations were provided. The first was near Rumfan Gwamna, some twelve miles north of Jos along the main Jos-Zaria road. This site was judged suitable and healthy for the establishment of a mission station. The other option was in the neighborhood of Kachia or Zangon Kataf in Southern Zaria. Of the two places, only Rumfan Gwamna seemed to have been free for the Adventists to establish their station without any conflict with another mission. Despite the apparent advantages, the Adventists were less enthusiastic about the prospect of establishing a station there, due to the relatively sparse population, while the second site at Zangon Kataf was much more attractive. When the second alternative was conveyed to McClements, he wrote, "I shall be pleased to convey this information to our Board in London on my returning to England early in April. In the meantime, one of our representatives will investigate the location to which you have referred and undoubtedly call and see you."[55]

52. Shankar, *Who Shall Enter Paradise?*, 329.

53. Barnes, "'Evangelization,'" 436.

54. Monsell, 1931; National Archives of Kaduna Zar. Prof. 41, 1932.

55. National Archives of Kaduna, "Minutes," in the Memorandum No 14432/11, "1 March 1931, on Seventh-Day Adventist Mission—Establishment of."

In response, Hyde undertook a visit to see the resident of Zaria and expressed his desire to proceed to Zangon Kataf, which he considered more suitable for mission. Accordingly, when Hyde inspected the site on April 20, 1931, he submitted an application for a certificate of occupancy. In the covering letter to the D. O. he stated:

> We are generally known as the "Seventh-Day Adventist Mission." Our property in Nigeria is held under a Power of Attorney granted by the General Conference Corporation of Seventh-Day Adventists, of Washington D.C. . . . Our building lease is required for purposes of erecting the following buildings: European Residence; Houses for Native Assistance; Mission Dispensary; School for Pagan Children; and a Hospital. . . . It is our purpose to commence the Medical side of our work in a Dispensary, and to grow on into a Hospital as the work increases. Hence our request for 15 acres of land and for 5 years in which to complete the buildings. . . . It is possible that experience may indicate a more suitable site for the permanent Hospital. . . . All this, however is only a possibility. . . . Trusting that you will find everything in order, and that nothing will arise to cause undue delay in the completion of this matter.[56]

Unfortunately, many problems encumbered the processing and granting of the application. On receiving it, the D. O. of Zaria forwarded it to the resident, explaining that the matter had been discussed with the assistant D. O. Mr. Roberts, who thought that there was no objection.[57] Indeed, Roberts discharged his work very well when he was instructed to visit the site of the application to

---

56. Hyde, Seventh-Day Adventist Mission Nigerian Branch, P.O. Box 19, Ibadan, a letter addressed to: District Officer i/c Emirate Division, Zaria, April 20th, 1931, National Archives of Kaduna Zar. Prof. C. 402 vol. 2.

57. National Archives of Kaduna, Zar. Prof. C. 402 vol. 2. A similar positive response was given by the emir of Zazzau, who expressed his willingness to allow it so long as the mission only worked among the "pagan" population. Immediately after the application was received, a request to visit the Katabawa was made by the "SIM of Kagoro." F. Daniel, Acting Resident, Zaria Province, Intelligent Report Zaria 1929–32:65.

make sure that there would be no problems with the local population. In his report, Roberts stated: "I have inspected this site with Katuka. At the moment it is a farmland, but no hardship will occur to the local natives if it is handed over."[58] Roberts also indicated that Katuka agreed with the plans of building a hospital and the mission's focus among non-Muslims.

But the accompanying district officer's note also called the resident's attention to another application from the SIM requesting permission to work in the same sphere of influence, though no action had been taken. It was this clash of interest for Zangon Kataf that brought the Adventists and SIM into an unhealthy rivalry.[59]

Missionary Rivalry

Though the idea of creating spheres of influence was to prevent unhealthy rivalry and to minimize open confrontation between missionaries, the story on the ground was very different. It is a fact that wherever and whenever spheres of influence were created, either for the conduct of commerce and trade or for missionary enterprise, intense competition and clashes were inevitable. In the northern region of the Rivers Niger and Benue, there was a wide expanse of space among the non-Muslim societies for the early arrivals. Thus, there were no problems and no accounts of unhealthy rivalries among the missionaries. Over time, however, with an increase in the number of denominations and the expansion of their activities, available spheres of influence diminished significantly. This was the situation by 1931 when Adventists wished to missionize in Zangon Kataf. Since the response of the resident in Zaria was not positive, McClements' reply to the district officer in charge of Zaria Division indicates the intractable nature of the problem:

> 1. Your letter . . . dated 19th . . . came to me a few days ago, and I must admit being somewhat surprised at its

58. Roberts 1931: National Archives of Kaduna, Zar. Prof. 41, 1932.

59. Some scholars note that mission rivalry was not uncommon in the Nigerian mission field. See Ekechi, *Missionary Enterprise and Rivalry in Igboland*; Bassey, "Missionary Rivalry and Educational Expansion."

contents; however, I appreciate your thought in the matter of referring our application back to us before proceeding further with it.

2. We understood that the S.I.M. had a station at Kagoro in the Plateau Province, but we also understood that their work had not as yet extended to the Katab people.

3. As you know, we have been deeply impressed with the situation at Zangon Katab and the large tribe of Pagan people there amongst whom little or nothing has been done along Missionary lines thus far. It seems to us that in working for these people and building up a medical work there we could have a good location, and would not be so likely to clash with other Missions as we might elsewhere.

4. We would therefore be glad if you would proceed with our application for the site at Zangon Kataf, as it seems to be the best opening we have seen so far.

5. I am sending a copy of your letter by this mail to our Mission Board, and also to Mr. Hyde who is in England at present, with the request that they cable me if they advise us to withdraw the application, in which case I would immediately communicate with you.[60]

On the receipt of this letter, the officials in Zaria responded: "Resident/I suggest that we defer action on this application for a C. of O. until we receive the communication promised . . . and until we know more about the intention of the S.I.M. with regard to Zangon Kataf."[61] From the provincial office, the resident of Zaria communicated the decision of SIM to McClements:

1. I have the honour to inform you that I have received a letter from the [SIM] in reply to a letter from me informing them that you had applied, on behalf of your mission, for a site at Zongon Katab.

2. After expressing regret that your Mission has made the application they put the following points:

---

60. McClements, "Progress in the Nigerian Mission Field," 9; National Archives of Kaduna (N.A.K.) Zar. Prof. 41, 1932.

61. N.A.K. Zar. Prof. 41, 1932.

(a). The Katab people speak the same language as the Kagoros (amongst whom they are at present working in Plateau Province) and intermarry. The Katab extend to within eight miles of Kagoro and are different only in name.
(b). Zongon Katab lies between their stations at Kurmin Musa and Dama Kasuwa while Kagoro is only a few miles to the south.
(c). That they made application for a site at Zongon Katab three years ago, but that before definite action was taken those who were to have opened the station were invalided and the project was dropped for the time. That they have never abandoned the idea of eventually working among the Katab tribe and that it is a natural field for their evangelists.
(d). That confusion will arise if two missions work in such close proximity among a tribe with a limited population.
3. In view of the above I shall be glad to know if you will reconsider your proposal to open a Mission Centre at Zongon Katab.[62]

By this time, reorganization had taken place within the Adventist Mission. They changed their name to Nigerian Union Mission of Seventh-day Adventists. McClements responded indicating his displeasure over the situation. He seemed to be irritated over the fact that Adventists were not consulted on the issue of spheres of influence:

> I am in receipt of your letter . . . and note what you state regarding the attitude of the Sudan Interior Mission to our opening up work at Zangon Katab. We, too, regret very much that the SIM should take up this attitude towards our proposed work in that district. As expressed in my previous letter . . . we feel very much drawn to the Zangon Katab. The Mission Board at home has been deeply impressed by the report we sent on our return from Zaria in April and they are anxious for us to locate there and build up a Medical Mission centre.

---

62. N.A.K. Zar. Prof. 41, 1932.

> In view of the fact that our interests were not consulted when spheres of influence were allocated by the S.I.M. and other Missions—though we have been operating within the Northern Provinces for the past sixteen years—it is probable we should have encountered similar opposition had we decided upon the other districts suggested.
>
> We certainly desire to work as much as possible in harmony with other Missions, but, after giving careful consideration to all the points raised, we would still feel very reluctant to withdraw our application.[63]

Having analyzed the two positions by the Adventists and SIM, the resident of Zaria wrote to the secretary of Northern Provinces, lamenting in the end that, "in the circumstances there would appear to be no alternative but inform the Seventh-day Adventists that their application cannot be granted."[64]

By this time, Hyde had already established himself at Zangon Kataf in the hope of building permanent headquarters on this site for the Adventist Mission work in Northern Nigeria. In a progress report on the Nigerian front, McClements enthusiastically wrote to the Adventist public, citing God's providence in doing medical mission in Zagon Kataf: "The people of this area . . . are anxious for us to open a dispensary or hospital here, and have given us a large tract of land for this purpose. The English officials also welcome us into the district with our medical work. So we believe the Lord has been directing us to this section of the northern provinces in a special manner."[65]

Unaware of the Adventist enthusiasm, the secretary of Northern Provinces conveyed the decision of the lieutenant governor to the resident of Zaria, saying, "It is desirable that Missionary bodies should agree among themselves to avoid interference in their respective spheres of influence. . . . I am to say that you should represent this point to the Seventh-day Adventist Mission who in

---

63. McClements, "Progress," 8; N.A.K. Zar. Prof. 41, 1932.
64. McClements, "Progress," 8.
65. McClements, "Progress," 9.

the circumstances might be prepared to reconsider their application, and that you understand there would be no objection."[66]

In further communication on this matter, the resident of Zaria informed McClements that the authorities did not approve the Adventist application for Zangon Kataf. At the same time, the resident of Plateau was also contacted to confirm about Rumfan Gwamna. However, there was no need for confirmation because McClements and Hyde had earlier seen the resident, Mr. C. A. N. Clarke, on the issue. Since the SIM claimed the area of Zangon Kataf as one of their spheres of influence, the Adventists were advised to withdraw their application. In Clarke's view, the application was withdrawn immediately.[67]

However, the problem persisted. On September 7, 1931, McClements wrote to the resident of Zaria, inquiring about their application for Zagon Kataf.[68] In his reply, the resident asked McClements to reconsider the problem of the site in view of the strong points previously raised by Mr. Playfair of the SIM. Since he was not prepared to accept defeat, McClements visited the resident in Zaria on November 10. However, he was advised to settle the matter with the SIM. The prospects for other sites at Kauru, Birnin Gwari, and Kachia were also discussed, none of which were acceptable to McClements.

Undeniably, there was an intense rivalry between the Adventists and SIM over the spheres of influence, particularly in the southern part of Zaria Province. Seeing no headway, McClements decided to go in person to discuss the matter with the director of SIM in Jos and promised to communicate the outcome with the resident of Zaria. Despite the intensity of the rivalry, the two bodies finally resolved the issue and settled their problem by demarcating boundaries for their respective spheres of operations. After the meeting, on November 20, McClements wrote:

66. Thompstone, Secretary Northern Provinces, to Resident, Zaria Province, on Seventh Day Adventist Mission, August 27, 1931, : N.A.K. Zar. Prof. 41, 1932.

67. Clarke, 1931: N.A.K. Zar. Prof. 41, 1932.

68. McClements, "Progress," 9; : N.A.K. Zar. Prof. 41, 1932.

> This is to inform you that we have had several friendly discussions with the Director of the S.I.M. and have agreed to withdraw our application for site at Zangon Kataf in their favor. Mr. Playfair . . . has assured us that the S.I.M. have no intention of pushing further into the Zaria Province unless we fail to occupy it.
>
> I understand Mr. Playfair is writing you immediately to confirm this. We are planning to make a further survey of the southern part of the Province with a view to making a new application. . . . We expect to call and see you in about ten days' time.[69]

As expected, Playfair, in confirming the above, reported that the Adventists had withdrawn their application for Zagon Katab. He also stated that the SIM had no intention of pushing further into Zaria Province as McClements had stated.[70]

McClements returned to Ibadan and reported the matter to the board, where his withdrawal of the application was discussed and ratified. He then wrote to the resident of Zaria affirming the final decision of the Mission on the matter: "I am writing with reference to our former application for a site in Zaria Province and wish to state that we have decided, after careful consideration and consultation . . . to open our work in Jos Division. We will therefore, for the moment, withdraw our application for Zangon-Kataf and await another suitable opening where we can utilize the experience gained in Jos."[71] With the bitter rivalries behind them, Adventists then embraced the task of choosing a suitable alternative site upon which to develop a permanent center for their operation in Northern Nigeria.

Establishing a Permanent Mission Station

The long-drawn-out contest over the sphere of influence with the SIM caused unnecessary delays in the establishment of a

69. Playfair 1931: N.A.K. Zar. Prof. 41, 1932.
70. McClements, 1931: N.A.K. Zar. Prof. 41, 1932.
71. McClements, 1932: N.A.K. Zar. Prof. 41, 1932.

permanent base of operations for the Adventist mission. The discussions took almost a year before the mission could turn its attention to Jengre, in Jere District of Jos Division, without fear of clashes. The presence of the Adventist station in this area confined the activities of SIM around Zabolo some twenty miles away from Jengre. Hyde and his wife, a trained nurse, relocated to Jengre around December 31, 1932. They brought along a Hausa man who had been recruited to assist with dispensary work while at Zangon Kataf. Led by Mrs. Hyde, the dispensary, which later became the Jengre SDA Hospital, provided an avenue to reach the people in the area who were in dire need of medical treatment.

There was an epidemic of jigger during the first year of the stations' establishment, and the effectiveness of the treatment given to those who attended the mission station drew quite many people. From December 1931 to March 1932, a temporary booth of woven grass (*zana*) was built where sick people received treatment, and where Bible lessons and Sabbath worship were initially conducted.[72]

Having firmly established the mission work at Jengre, Hyde was then prepared to launch Adventism in and around the villages of the area. Among the first people who demonstrated keen interest in the Adventist mission work were Mallam Lamba Kakwi and Kaji Dariya. These two had previously been in contact with SIM missionaries operating from Jos. With the establishment of the Adventist station very close to them, they were more than happy to embrace the new Sabbath teachings.

Hyde depended initially on Kakwi and Dariya for the expansion of the Adventist mission to the surrounding villages.[73] He understood the need to have a knowledge of the Hausa and Amo languages and labored to build relationships in his community. Notable was the relationship he had with the Kakwi family. The four sons of Kakwi—Lamba, Mayang, Filibus, and Simon—became his "disciples" and worked as pioneers in their community. They all later became Adventist ministers. Before Hyde left for

72. Hyde, Fieldwork (Watford, 1994).
73. Maigadi, *Adventist Church in Northern Nigeria*, 38–44.

Sierra Leone in 1942, a semiformal school where adult education was emphasized had begun. Hyde was replaced by L. W. Normington, who ushered in a second phase of Adventist mission in the North of Nigeria as has been explored in chapter 2.

SUMMARY AND CONCLUSION

This chapter has argued that the reason for the apparent difficulties faced by early Adventist missionaries in the North of Nigeria can be hinged on three factors. Their relative lateness to the missionary scene in Nigeria, combined with the colonial policy that restricted Christian mission activities in the North, delayed the Adventist mission. By the time the restrictions were relaxed, other Christian missionaries had developed cordial relationships with the colonial authorities, agreeing on several policies, chief of which was the spheres of influence for mission activities.

By the time Adventist missionaries arrived, other Christian missions were firmly established in Nigeria. Unaware and reluctant to consult other missionaries, Adventist missionaries were pushed into an unhealthy rivalry with the SIM in a bid to establish a permanent mission station. This caused an unnecessary delay that could have been avoided had Adventists arrived earlier. Moreover, if Adventists had been willing to consult other mission bodies initially, they would have learned about the colonial politics that ruled the missionary scene of Northern Nigeria.

While this chapter has given insight into mission rivalry, which was not uncommon in the Nigerian mission field,[74] its focus was on the history of the beginnings of the Adventists as an unlikely mission group, which does not appear frequently in scholarly works on mission historiography in Nigeria. This chapter has attempted to fill this lacuna which has remained unmapped in the story of Christian mission in Nigeria.

---

74. Ekechi, *Missionary Enterprise and Rivalry in Igboland*; Bassey, "Missionary Rivalry and Educational Expansion."

Chapter 4

The Encounter of Adventist Missionaries with Indigenous Issues in Nigeria from 1900 to the 1940s

THIS FOURTH CHAPTER[1] EXPLORES the intricate and complex relationships of Adventist missionaries with indigenous issues during their mission work in Nigeria. It argues that despite their relative success, the approach of the missionaries to indigenous culture was colored by points of conflict and the stark difference to their vision of Christ's parousia. As a result, indigenous issues like the position of women in the society and public matters, polygamy, and charismatism in worship were divested of cultural significance and in some cases demonized and replaced with Adventist alternatives. Preparing converts for the second coming of Christ meant the disengagement of any cultural practice that seemingly turned the focus of converts away from the imminence of the kingdom of the otherworldly.

1. Originally published as "Preparing Converts for the Second Coming of Christ."

The Adventist conviction of the imminent return of Christ pushed them to the far ends of the world. This is a fact that cannot be overemphasized. That conviction brought Adventist missionaries to Africa with an "invitation to join an eschatological community"[2] that proclaimed the three angels' messages. However, an end-time proclamation also meant an encounter with challenges of various indigenous cultures and practices. How Adventist missionaries dealt with complex cultural issues while preaching the future Christ event still remains an engaging academic subject in mission history.

There are several scholarly works which analyze the encounter of Western missionaries with indigenous cultural issues in Africa. Issues like power relations, colonialism, ancestor worship, and rites of passage have played significant roles in the discourse. While many have viewed Western missionaries as soulmates of colonialism, others have focused on the positive contributions of missionaries to the development and civilization of African cultures and societies.[3] Among Adventists in general, this discourse is nearly nonexistent. An exception is Stefan Höschele's *Christian Remnant—African Folk Church*, which analyzes Adventist missionary engagements with the traditional Tanzanian culture among other themes.[4] When it comes to Nigeria, there are only two main works that highlight the encounter of Christianity and African cultures.[5]

Consequently, the key question to be explored in this chapter is how Adventist missionaries dealt with indigenous issues during their mission work in Nigeria. As will be shown in this chapter, in the face of the imminent parousia, the missionary approach to indigenous culture was marked by points of conflict and stark difference. It must be maintained that not all elements of culture were

2. Bosch, *Transforming Mission*, 123.

3. Kaplan, "Africanization of Missionary Christianity"; Samson, "Problem of Colonialism"; Fiedler, "Christian Missions and Western Colonialism."

4. Höschele, *Christian Remnant*, 259–362.

5. Kuranga, "Seventh-day Adventism in Western Nigeria"; Alalade, *Limiting Factors*.

demonized or discouraged. Those practices that were seemingly considered harmless were even used for the purposes of mission propagation. For instance, the ancient talking drum, an element of communication across Nigeria's various ethnic groups, was used to call people to worship on Sabbath morning.[6] In some mission reports, aspects of culture like hospitality and the manner of singing have been praised. In fact, one female Adventist missionary, Mary J. Vine, once compared the manner in which native Abuans (a tribe in Southern Nigeria) learned and sang Adventist hymns to the type of singing that may emanate from the 144,000 in Revelation.[7]

This chapter is a historical reflection on and analysis of the subject of Adventist missionizing in Nigeria from 1900 to the 1940s with reference to three crucial cultural issues: the position of women in society, polygamy, and charismatic tendencies in worship. After highlighting the peculiar context of Nigeria, the nature and approaches of the missionaries will be outlined. This will pave the way for the three case studies that form the major inquiry in this chapter.

ESTABLISHING AN ADVENTIST MISSION IN NIGERIA: CONTEXT AND BEGINNINGS

Here the lateness of Adventism to Nigeria is reiterated as earlier explored in chapter 3. The reader should be assured that the reiteration here does not amount to redundancy. Rather, the points are reiterated for the sake of clarity and contextualization of some of the new insights that are explored in this chapter. Having made that caveat, we now progress with further insights into the late coming of the Adventist mission enterprise to Nigeria.

While the earliest Christian mission to Nigeria can be traced back to the sixteenth century[8] and Protestants arrived in

6. Maxwell, "Widening Horizons."

7. Vine, "New Song."

8. "The first Portuguese ships anchored off the cost of the west-central Africa kingdom of Kongo in 1483. Catholicism survived, in an indigenized form, until the late nineteenth century, when a new wave of missionary activity began. It was introduced into the Niger Delta kingdom of Warri in the 1570s;

the late 1840s, Adventists arrived at the beginning of the 1900s and officially established their mission in 1914. 1914 was the year Lord Frederick D. Lugard of the British Empire amalgamated the Northern and Southern Protectorates to form today's Nigeria, a product of British colonization. The colonization of Nigeria was a prolonged development.[9] In the case of Nigeria, Falola and Heaton have argued that colonization "brought under the sole rule of the United Kingdom previously independent states that had been interconnected commercially and to some extent culturally over the previous centuries, but had not experienced political unification of any kind."[10] Before the colonial period there had existed nation-states of the Hausa-Fulani, Oyo, Ijebu, Ife, Kanem Bornu, the many Igbo kingdoms, the Benin Kingdom, etc. Hence, the 1914 amalgamation succeeded in lumping together several nation-states and kingdoms.[11] No wonder Sir Hugh Clifford, governor general of Nigeria (1919–25), once dismissed the idea of Nigeria as a nation: He argued Nigeria is "a collection of independent Native states, separated from one another by great distances, by differences of history and traditions and by ethnological, racial, tribal, political, social and religious barriers."[12] These barriers seen by Sir Hugh Clifford in the 1920s also bring to mind the description of Nigeria by Ken Post and Michael Vickers as a "conglomerate society" where citizens struggle to balance various social identifications.[13] It was into this environment that Adventism entered. Undeniably, the arrival of Adventism to Nigeria happened in two phases.[14] The first phase comprised the mission attempts of commissioned laymen and self-supporting missionaries. The first attempt to establish the denomination in Nigeria was carried out

---

despite long periods without missionaries, it endured until the mid-eighteenth century." Isichei, *History of Christianity*, 45.

9. Falola and Heaton, *History of Nigeria*, 109.
10. Falola and Heaton, *History of Nigeria*, 109.
11. Falola and Oyeniyi, *Nigeria*, 23–67.
12. Coleman, *Nigeria*, 194.
13. Post and Vickers, *Structure and Conflict*.
14. Wogu, "Trailblazers."

by James M. Hyatt, a Black layman missionary from the United States. Hyatt had been working in Ghana and Sierra Leone and went to Nigeria between 1906 and 1907. Around the same time, in the very South of Nigeria, a young Ghanaian Adventist, Sydney Hayford, was employed as colonial government schoolmaster in Bonny. Simultaneously, he began doing some Adventist mission work and introduced Benjamin I. Tikili to Adventist beliefs. Tikili and his group of growing believers remained "Adventists" until an official Adventist missionary, Jesse C. Clifford, arrived in Aba in 1923. Thence, they officially became Adventists after baptism. Tikili later became an ordained Adventist minister in 1924.

Contrastingly, the second phase of the Adventist mission started around 1913 with ordained and commissioned missionaries who built upon the work started in the first phase. This phase brought David C. Babcock together with three other West African workers: R. P. Dauphin (an ordained minister), Samuel D. Morgue, and James J. Hamilton (commissioned licentiates). After the Nigerian mission was officially organized in 1913, the Babcock team arrived in 1914, focusing their attention to the West of Nigeria while based in Ibadan. In 1923, the Southern part of Nigeria got its official missionary, Jesse C. Clifford, who got in touch with Tikili in Aba, from where Adventism spread in the South of Nigeria.[15] By the mid-1930s, Adventists had touched the major regions of Nigeria. The mission work was now established. The question was how to maintain and grow the burgeoning church in the most populous Black nation of the world with its diverse cultural and contextual issues.

MISSION THROUGH INSTITUTIONAL ORGANIZATIONS

As the 1940s set in, Adventism experienced further growth as it used institutions for missionary purposes. George Knight, a key Adventist historian, has argued that the Adventist denominational mission has always been managed structurally through

---

15. Wogu, "Trailblazers," 1–8.

such organizations: The formation of publishing, administrative, educational, and medical institutions is a distinguishing feature of Adventist mission. It was a feature which began, though unintentionally, early in the church's history and was replicated in various mission fields. The use of those four types of institutions as mission strategy is what George Knight calls "Adventism's missiological quadrilateral."[16]

Specifically, in Nigeria, Adventism's missiological quadrilateral was replicated to a large extent. By the 1940s, Adventism in Nigeria operated educational (notably: Teacher's Training School, Ibadan), health (Ile-Ife Hospital and Jengre Hospital, 1947), and printing institutions (Advent Printing Press, Oke-Bola, 1935). These early institutions contributed to the growth of the church as it supported evangelistic efforts and Bible study classes. They not only provided services of education, health, and printing resources; they were avenues for training new Adventist converts. In addition, they meant job opportunities for a significant number of these converts. In essence, missionary Adventism in Nigeria began functioning as a holistic movement where the spiritual, mental, social, and physical/psychological welfare of the members was catered to. This was not unusual for Protestant missions in those days; other mission organizations also built schools and hospitals alongside their evangelistic mission activities. Nevertheless, the Adventist movement in Nigeria clearly mirrored principles of American Adventism.

ENCOUNTERING AND DEALING WITH INDIGENOUS ISSUES

Having explored the major approaches of Adventist missionaries especially early in the history of Adventism in Nigeria, it is important to note that they were successful in gaining converts.[17] Nevertheless, the missionaries at the time faced tremendous challenges

---

16. Knight, *Fat Lady and the Kingdom*, 81.
17. Izima, *Brief History*, 43.

in maintaining the established mission. In their encounter with culture, Adventist missionaries faced peculiar complexities in relation to indigenous practices of their converts. This section will focus on three main challenges that arose.

The Place of Women in Society and in Adventist Mission Praxis

The following case study of the Igbo, among whom Adventism progressed steadily in the 1930s and up to the 1960s, shows that the important position of women in society was not taken seriously by Adventist missionaries. Igbo women had a history of battling male oppression through communal efforts. Moreover, Igbo women played a powerful social, political, and economic role in society. They formed political, social, and economic systems or institutions for governing their own issues in the Igbo traditional society.[18] However, colonialism and Christian missions apparently did not recognize this fact. While British colonial authorities excluded women from political power through the indirect rule system, Christian missionaries often had their own agenda for women.

As much as Christian missionaries made education a priority for their converts, according to Van Allen, the purpose of educating girls was to train them largely "to be Christian wives and mothers, not for jobs or for citizenship."[19] She states that missionaries

> were not necessarily against women's participation in politics—clergy in England, as in America, could be found supporting women's suffrage. But in Africa their concern was the church, and for the church they needed Christian families. Therefore, Christian wives and mothers, not female political leaders, was the missions' aim.[20]

---

18. Ezeigbo, "Traditional Women's Institutions in Igbo Society"; Nnoroviele, *Way People Live*.
19. Van Allen, "Aba Riots," 25.
20. Van Allen, "Aba Riots," 25.

This will be demonstrated in two ways: (1) the involvement of women in traditional rites and (2) women's participation in political and public order.

Women and Traditional Rites: The "Fattening" Rite of Passage

Adventist missionaries had similar views of training women and girls. William McClements, in his plea for funding to start a girls' school in Nigeria, decried the lack of educated Christian girls and especially the difficulty in finding Christian wives for the educated men of the mission. For McClements, when the Adventist young men left the training school to the mission field, there was need for "good intelligent Christian wives to help them in their homes and in their work."[21] Why was this so important for McClements and the Adventist mission in Nigeria? McClements claimed that the new crop of educated young men already had enough "degrading customs" to contend with outside their homes. These customs should not be seen in Adventist homes. Yet, as McClements complained, "homes of several of our brightest teachers are blighted by the influence of unsuitable wives."[22]

Citing the popular Igbo tradition of *Iru-mgbede* or *Nkpu* ("fattening"), young women of marriage age were separated for a period of six months before marriage. The women were to do no work but only eat and sleep as well as go through traditional education and initiation. McClements demonized the practice by asking, "How can young Adventist teachers take such wives; [*sic*] I am glad to say our members have taken their stand against this heathenish practice, but still things are not what they should be."[23] Hence the need for an Adventist girls' school. Yet McClements and other Adventist missionaries[24] failed to understand

---

21. McClements, "Nigeria Union Mission," 5.
22. McClements, "Nigeria Union Mission," 5.
23. McClements, "Nigeria Union Mission," 5.
24. Vine, "Marriage in the Ibo Country." The rite of passage was not just heathen or degrading; Vine saw the whole elements and practices attached to Nigerian marriage as "ugly," "uncivilized," or without "enchantment" as in England.

that *Iru-mgbede* or *Nkpu* was a rite of passage. It was one of the most famous pre-marriage preparations where participants were specifically given marriage instructions.[25] Instead, Mary Vine saw the rite as an ill-treatment of young women. She argued that some were made to endure the practice for six months if they could afford it. In this vein, any girl who could only partake in the rite for a month was "more fortunate, though she doesn't realize it, only being subjected to it for one month."[26]

Obviously, the lack of cultural understanding is apparent in the portrayal of this cultural practice. These missionaries were confronted with the otherness of an alien culture which they must have unconsciously regarded as heathen or degrading when compared to the ideals of their Western civilization. In reality, degrading words like "heathen" or "pagan" were popular in the missionaries' *zeitgeist*. Yet, if Adventist missionaries had forgone their ethnocentrism and undertaken a careful investigation of the practice in discussion, they might have concluded otherwise. The rite was based on a holistic philosophy that gave a single woman ample time to be prepared by older women through intellectual, emotional, and physical education for the status of becoming a married woman. As Dioka concluded, during the period of fattening, the women were "formally taught the virtues of womanhood, fidelity to husband, pregnancy rules and childcare, house craft and other necessary requirements for a happy married life."[27]

The attempt of creating a substitute for a rite that was viewed as ineffective and incompatible to Adventism is similar to Steven Kaplan's conception of "Christianization."[28] Kaplan used the term to "characterize those cases in which missionaries sought to create

---

25. The best treatment of this cultural practice is Onwuzurigbo, "Igbo Marriage and Family Life."

26. Vine, "Marriage in the Ibo Country," 11–12.

27. Dioka, "Marriage in Igboland," 3.

28. Christianization was one element in the typology of Kaplan developed to show how Western missionaries responded to African indigenous cultures. Others were toleration, assimilation, translation, acculturation, and incorporation.

Christian versions of traditional African rites and practices."[29] Kaplan's treatment shows that advocates of this process were not full supporters of traditional practices. They acknowledged the valuable social and educational functions of the rites. Western missionaries subscribed to this process to cleanse and purify some practices resulting in eliminating the bad and substituting the good. Consequently, the process ensured that "the form generally remained African, the content became Christian."[30]

By way of contrast, the Adventist version of Christianization saw no positive value in the fattening rite. Hence, a complete alternative with recourse to Adventist education was proffered as the best solution. Therefore, not only were the missionaries wrong in hastily demeaning and vilifying this cultural practice; they glossed over an enviable opportunity to assimilate a good practice into their mission education program. Instead of appreciating the tradition, the missionaries had an agenda that saw a replacement for this "degrading custom" among Igbo women with Adventist education. By so doing they were creating a system that served as substitute subculture which had its own religio-cultural ethos.

Women and Public Order: The Aba Women Riots

Secondly, to the extent that women were the majority of the converts to Christianity, missionaries may have conceived women's role in society to be submissive even though indigenous women protested against unfair authorities. For instance, around December 1929, when Jesse Clifford returned from furlough in England, the Adventist mission buildings in Aba were temporarily used to house injured refugees as a result of the Women's Riot that had just erupted in November of that year. The riots led by women were the first major challenge to British colonial authority in Nigeria and British West Africa. They began as anti-tax protests by women who were upset with the colonial authorities' plans to impose

---

29. Kaplan, "Africanization," 17.
30. Kaplan, "Africanization," 17.

direct taxes on Igbo market women. This resulted in the massive opposition of women which came to be known as the "Women's War" among Nigerians and "Aba Riots" among the British.[31] By November and December of 1929, women from Owerri, Aba, and Calabar had looted factories and destroyed native court buildings and properties, including the homes of those associated with native courts.[32]

According to Falola and Heaton, the fact that the Women's War was organized and carried out by women who did not even have access to education at that time was an "indication of how frustrated average Nigerians were with the colonial regime and its puppet indirect rulers"[33] who were men. The event showed and illustrated the "capacity of average Nigerians to organize and voice their opposition to colonial policy despite the obstacles."[34] It is also an identifier of the political and social power controlled by women during these colonial periods. The women protests were one of the most formidable avenues for fostering anticolonial resistance. They are now widely seen as a turning point in the trajectory of anticolonial resistance[35] which in many ways slipped into the Christian missions. The many schisms of the 1930s which were locally led and resulted in several new indigenous churches, especially in Igboland, testify to this fact.

What remains relevant from the 1929 event is that as a result of the war, colonial authorities began recognizing women even as warrant chiefs as well as members in the native courts. It is not

---

31. Before the 1929 event, a census had been conducted in 1926 to determine who was eligible to pay tax in the Southeast region. In 1928, an assistant district officer in the Owerri Province ordered local warrant chiefs to conduct a follow-up census. In the process, "women in the region feared that a new census meant they were soon to be taxed as well. Already burdened with supporting families and helping men to pay their taxes, the women of Southeastern Nigeria held mass demonstrations and spread the protests throughout the regions." Falola and Heaton, *History of Nigeria*, 133.

32. Falola and Heaton, *History of Nigeria*, 133.

33. Falola and Heaton, *History of Nigeria*, 133.

34. Falola and Heaton, *History of Nigeria*, 133.

35. Falola and Heaton, *History of Nigeria*, 135.

certain whether Adventist missionaries joined the bandwagon to appreciate these types of local initiatives from women or not. What is sure is the denouncing of the 1929 event.

Clifford, leader of the Adventist mission in the Southeast, reported negatively on the event. According to Clifford, the 1929 event was a "mob, consisting of thousands of native women" who went around the district "destroying the post office, looting the stores, releasing the prisoners, and destroying the houses of their chiefs. The markets are closed, for they rob all they meet, and Aba is like a dead town."[36]

Again, what we see is a hasty conclusion of the priorities of indigenous women. However, there is a more important cause for the way Clifford sounded in his report. Clifford's emphasis on public order and the disruption of social and political activities stemmed from his concerns about the future prospects of his work as an Adventist missionary:

> It seems rather trying to be thus held up after furlough when there is so much to be done, but we hope it will soon be over, and that it will work out to the advancement of the cause. Truly we must work now, or our "little time of peace" will soon be in the past.[37]

The missionary's portrayal of the women uprising betrayed his pacifist views and perhaps his implicit support of colonial structures. Nevertheless, what really bothered Clifford was the fact that the uprising brought the advancement of the Adventist cause to a standstill. As a result of the activities of some unscrupulous elements in the society, this missionary was hit with the inability to go about his urgent missionary duties of proclaiming Christ's parousia. This was a setback to a missionary who took the urgency of Christ's soon return to heart. This perspective of imminence is easily detected in his mission reports. After establishing the mission in Aba, Clifford began a Bible class where he primarily taught

---

36. Clifford, "Troublous Times in West Africa," 8.
37. Clifford, "Troublous Times in West Africa," 8.

his students about the Sabbath and the second coming of Jesus.[38] Moreover, when he moved to Ghana, Clifford left a mission legacy colored with "a high focus on eschatology and the second coming of Christ."[39]

Therefore, Clifford's eschatology was a typically pessimist premillennialism, as Rick Langer would term it, that "looks ahead to a rising world crisis that will only be averted by the return of Christ Himself. Things do not get better and better before the return of Christ, but quite the opposite."[40] As Langer further argues, this kind of thinking impeded cultural engagement. Thus, Clifford's denouncement may have been a result of his preoccupation with an eschatology that encouraged an optimism of the otherworldly rather than this-worldly. It shows that to a large extent some Adventist missionaries seem to have been culturally disengaged. Understanding the nature and significance of the women's uprising would have been an avenue to adequately incorporate the culture and ethos of indigenous women into the Adventist system in Nigeria, but this opportunity was missed.

Polygamy

In many other cases, Adventists neither engaged with the culture of the mission field nor built on those converts who held the Sabbath truth and seemed closer to their own faith and beliefs. For instance, around 1930, after Tikili was ordained,[41] Clifford and especially Tikili sought converts in the hinterlands of the Brass Tribe and Abua, a riverine area of the South known as the Niger Delta.[42] In those hinterlands, Adventist workers met with other Sabbath-keeping groups. One was the Church of Christ Seventh Day. Clifford was faced with the dilemma of accepting this group

---

38. Babalola, *Sweet Memories of Our Pioneers*, 81.
39. Owusu-Mensa, "Clifford, Jesse."
40. Langer, "Kingdom Integration."
41. Clifford, "Like a Grain of Mustard Seed."
42. Clifford, "Camp-Meetings in Southern Nigeria."

of Sabbatarians as foundational members of the Adventist Church there. In other places, a number of indigenous Sabbath-keeping groups were incorporated into Adventist congregations.[43] However, Clifford decided otherwise. Why did he make such a decision? Since most of the Sabbatarians "were polygamists and engaged in other strange practices and customs,"[44] they did not stand a chance of being incorporated into the body of Adventists.

On the issue of polygamy, Clifford's decision was understandable since Adventist missionaries, like many other Christians of the period, were not supporters of the practice. In 1921, after Malcolm N. Campbell, then British Union Conference president, took a tour of West Africa, he condemned and discouraged polygamy as the "most difficult institution" faced by missionaries. He encouraged workers to continue to act under deep conviction of the truth so that converts would make the adequate sacrifice and abandon the practice.[45] McClements not only saw the practice as the greatest hindrance to mission; plurality of wives was "the curse of Africa."[46] In fact, the General Conference Session of 1926 had taken an action not to admit any man living in polygamy into the fellowship of the church.[47] Hence, the treatment of the practice, its practitioners, and, especially, polygamous converts by Adventists was somewhat inconsiderate. Two cases are explored in this respect.

In the first case, Clifford praised a convert named Sampson who resisted the temptation of going into polygamous marriage by inheritance. In a mission report, Clifford claimed that after the death of Sampson's father, the Igbo native law compelled him to take his father's inheritance which included the young wives. However,

---

43. Maxwell, "Widening Horizons," 1.
44. Alao, *90 Years*, 34.
45. Campbell, "West African Problems."
46. McClements, "Missionary Problems in Nigeria."
47. Cormack, "Polygamy and Marriage Relationship." See original decision in "Polygamy," General Conference Session Action, 1926, Box 3811, subject: Polygamy, General Conference Archives, Silver Spring, Maryland, USA.

Sampson refused to do this, and chose to lose his father's inheritance rather than be forced to go contrary to God's will. When he had taken this stand, the women themselves used every persuasion to induce him to take them, but he stood firm. Finally, after a long period of persecution, they left him alone.[48]

In another polygamous case, William, a rich man, had been married with five wives before becoming an Adventist. When he accepted the Adventist faith, he and all his family joined the church. However, while William desired baptism and the opportunity to preach the Adventist message, this was not possible since the leaders refused. Eventually, Williams decided to find husbands for his four wives. He did find three young men from the Adventist Church to marry his former wives. Unfortunately, this led the women to leave the Adventist faith because they saw the transfer of husbands as a disgrace to them in their traditional society. They did not deserve divorce. Vine explained that

> William's heart failed him. The salvation of those women meant much to him, and of the two wives that remained, if any one of the five had been dearer to him than the rest, she whom he must now send away was the one. A good, faithful woman, she, a sort of self-constituted deaconess in the church. William wavered and prayed and prayed and wavered, and surely as a result of the praying, Sabinah herself made the decision. "It is not right that I should stay," said she, "only let me live in your compound until such time, William, as you have found another husband for me"—truly a noble course of action which rejoiced William's heart. But what was William's horror and surprise when Cordelia, his first and now only remaining wife, and hitherto quite faithful, grew tired of her drab existence as the lone mistress in her establishment, and went astray with other men.[49]

The two stories are fascinating illustrations of the complexity that arose in the missionary encounter with indigenous Nigerian

---

48. Clifford, "Message in the Niger Delta."
49. Vine, "Marriage in the Ibo Country," 15.

practices. In principle, polygamous converts were not accepted into Adventist congregation. However, we see a kind of tolerance with polygamous converts who seem to have been participating in Adventist rituals. What changed? By 1930, the 1926 General Conference action was changed. A new policy resolved that in places "where tribal customs subject a cast-off wife to lifelong shame and disgrace, even to the point of becoming common property," polygamists may be "admitted to baptism and the ordinances of the church and be recognized as probationary members."[50]

While the interesting dynamics of how this change came about at the Adventist top-tier body has been analyzed by Höschele,[51] insight from Kaplan's analysis of "missionary toleration" proves most helpful. Toleration was used by Kaplan to "characterize those cases in which missionaries agreed to accept the continued existence of certain African social customs" while maintaining their incompatibility with Christianity.[52] As a fitting example, Kaplan alludes to polygamy which, in theory, most missionaries were opposed to. However, the practice was tolerated because of its extensive manifestation. This helps to understand the 1930 decision and the reasons why the polygamists were participating in Adventist practices. However, as Kaplan rightly observes, in respect to a tolerant attitude towards polygamy, "we should not be misled into reading decisions passed by a majority as if they had unanimous support."[53] Among Adventists, there was no unanimous support for the decision. As Höschele noted, although the 1930 resolution had a missiological strength, "its weakness was the lack of support by those engaged in missionary service."[54] Therefore, although a decision was made at the General Conference Headquarters back

50. Fall Council Action, 1930, 74–75, Box 3811, subject: Polygamy, General Conference Archives, Maryland, USA.

51. Höschele traces the reasons why the change came about especially through the intervention of "William H. Branson, the leader of the denomination's African region and later General Conference president." See Höschele, "To Baptize," 38–41.

52. Kaplan, "Africanization," 10.

53. Kaplan, "Africanization," 11.

54. Höschele, "To Baptize," 39.

home, those in the field had different opinions. Hence, while tolerating the polygamous converts as "probationary members," the missionaries ensured that such members were not fully "admitted to full membership unless or until circumstances change so as to leave them with only one companion."[55]

Nonetheless, deeper than issues of policy, polygamy was considered by missionaries as a hindrance to the Adventist vision. This turned the outlook of the missionaries from the social wellbeing of the converts, and the social and cultural significance of the practice, to the perceived conflictual barrier erected by polygamy. Therefore, while Clifford did not raise the question of who would take care of the former wives of Sampson's father or how they would fare, he was more interested in showing the general Adventist public, especially those in the West, back home, that the Adventist message was progressing such that young men in the church like Sampson had begun rejecting local customs and traditions while accepting Adventist ways of life.

In the case of William, while his place and position in society were lost, his place and position in the Adventist church was gained. As Vine reported, William

> had been a respected man because of his affluence; now he is nothing but extremely poor. Which illustrates very forcibly the unconverted Ibo woman's attitude of mind, and, incidentally, one of the greatest problems we missionaries have to face.[56]

Although this inquiry does not necessarily support polygamous practice, it is very easy to take sides and be sympathetic with William and his wives. Therefore, aside from sympathy, a number of questions which may not be fully explored comes to mind.

Since Vine was aware that having other women to talk to and cook with was a sign of good luck and prestige,[57] could she have intervened in trying to convince Cordelia, William's first wife, to

---

55. Fall Council Action, 1930, 74–75, Box 3811.
56. Vine, "Marriage in the Ibo Country," 15.
57. Mitchison, *Nigeria*, 82.

stay? Was Vine more interested in having a truly converted member, William, as a church member than losing all four women? Why was Vine not interested in the repercussions of William's action and his position in the society as well as the prestige of Cordelia? Unlike Clifford, Vine seems to have been interested in telling the Adventist public how difficult it was to work among "heathen" Igbo women who took pride in standing firmly in their traditional customs. Did this mean that the greatest opponent of the mission work was not polygamy[58] but unconverted women? Could there have been special missiological programs for those women? Or could the voices of those women in polygamous marriages have been taken seriously?

Possibly the issue of power relations was present. As was the case in several of those societies, social upward mobility was taken seriously. Therefore, questions in relation to William's actions come to mind. Was William acting on his own accord? Or was he merely interested in gaining position and power in the Adventist Church while substituting his status in society? These questions create more confusion than resolution. Answering these questions may lead to speculations since the story was only reported once and is therefore not well documented in the history of Adventism in Nigeria. In view of further explorations, it can be established that aside from hastily judging their host cultures, Adventist missionaries in Nigeria at that time failed to exhibit any form of flexibility towards local meanings in the face of misconceptions.

Spiritism or Indigenous Charismatics in the Church?

In the late 1930s, the Adventist Church was rocked by a schism in the Southeast of Nigeria. Unsurprisingly, before the schism, the Southeast region continued to have the influence and direct

---

58. This would seem to contrast with the 1925 claim of William McClements that polygamy was the greatest hindrance to the Adventist message. McClements, "Missionary Problems," 4. Other Christians had the same mindset. For instance, Anglican missionaries considered polygamy also as their greatest enemy. See Jones, "Missionaries' Position."

contribution of Tikili until the end of 1930s when he left Adventism, pulling several others with him. What led to the unfortunate disassociation of Tikili from the Adventist Church? In 1938, the world Adventist Sabbath School lesson featured topics related to "spiritual gifts" and the outpouring of the Holy Spirit at Pentecost in the first-quarter study guide.[59] During this time, the membership of the growing denomination in Aba believed in the imminent manifestation of "the latter rain." By July and August, a kind of "spirit movement" began. This charismatic movement saw several members claiming the power of the Spirit to see visions and dreams, heal the sick, raise the dead, make the lame to walk, etc. While others prophesied and spoke in tongues, others openly confessed their sins and were flogged publicly to gain forgiveness.[60]

Surprisingly, the movement brought about two conflicting opinions. While some saw those manifestations as satanic counterfeits, another group, most probably led by Tikili, the indigenous and influential pastor, believed the authenticity of the movement. When C. A. Bartlett, an Adventist regional leader, attended the workers' meeting in August, his lecture on "Try the Spirits Whether They Are of God" seemed to diminish or quell the movement's momentum and restored the much-cherished order known in Adventist circles. This may have come as an astounding move since McClements had earlier given an account of "Pentecostal Experiences in Nigeria" in 1937. McClements began his report with an ostentatious claim of "a new record of the Acts of the Holy Spirit." In narrating the deliverance of a convert from evil spirits, the healing of a woman through prayer who had been ill for nineteen years, and the conversion of a juju priest, McClements recounted how the Adventist message had exerted "a strong influence" in

---

59. Sabbath School Lesson Quarterly, First Quarter, 1938; Izima, *Brief History*, 23–24. The related topics included "The Church of God" (January 29, 1938), "Spiritual Gifts" (February 5, 1938), and most especially "Spiritual Gifts (Concluded)," which centered on the topic of Pentecost (February 12, 1938).

60. Izima, *Brief History*, 23–24.

Nigeria.⁶¹ Here again, a missionary seems to have been interested in the resulting effect of the Adventist message.

Implicitly, the direction of McClements' report painted an interesting picture. It seems to have claimed that the "Pentecostal experience" was possible only in the process of evangelization. Consequently, the Holy Spirit was limited to releasing those in bondage of evil spirits or giving power to the prayers of Adventist preachers. Thus, this view assumed that the work of the Holy Spirit was completed as soon as converts accepted Adventism. It is no wonder, then, that McClements solicited his readers "to pray for our workers and believers, that they may be filled with the Holy Spirit and prepared to do their part in finishing the working in Nigeria."⁶² Therefore, McClements' vision helps to explain Bartlett's lecture that branded the movement as counterfeit.

Nevertheless, if McClements saw the filling of the Holy Spirit as limited to finishing the mission work, Tikili's vision differed. The Holy Spirit's power can be bestowed upon those who have already professed Adventism. This can be evidenced in church life, during worship, and in the public engagements of God's people. Furthermore, the supernatural and charismatic elements that characterized the movement were not new to Tikili. Interestingly, in June of that year, Tikili recounted his conversion to Adventism. In the process, he told the Adventist public of his special gifts: visions and healing. Of his vision, "in 1924," Tikili claimed:

> The Lord showed me a night vision in which I was in a boat of pure gold, clear as glass. This boat took me to a certain village where there was a tree standing on the water's edge. Suddenly three eagles came and stood on its extensive boughs; and as I looked these birds said in a very loud voice, as of a cathedral bell, "Repent, for the world is coming to an end." This seemed to reach every part of the world. At these words the whole village turned

---

61. McClements, "Pentecostal Experiences in Nigeria."
62. McClements, "Pentecostal Experiences in Nigeria," 1.

out weeping. The boat stood there for about five minutes and turned me round without anybody rowing it.[63]

In respect to his healing power, Tikili maintained that God "has cured my diseases and has through me cured other men and women by prayer and a little first aid. I am known to many . . . as the 'doctor without medicine.' For by prayer I have given them release."[64] The account was republished in a number of other Adventist magazines like *Canadian Union Messenger, Lake Union Herald, Pacific Union Recorder,* and *Atlantic Union Gleaner.*

Unfortunately, the claim of the report cannot be fully assessed due to lack of historical data. Yet on a closer look, the report was an abridged version of Tikili's own account. In this vein, further insight could be made, though at the danger of speculation. Perhaps, Tikili had sought to give credence to the 1938 movement by resorting to his empirical and lived experiences from the time he was converted, called to pastoral ministry until the crisis of the late 1930s. If he had experienced visions and miraculous healing, then the ordinary Adventists could also experience the power and gifts of the Holy Spirit.

Moreover, in the worldview of many Africans, the cosmos is populated by benevolent and malevolent spirits. Malevolent spirits can cause misfortune, wreak havoc, and thwart progress in individual and communal lives. Being able to control the cosmos and knowing the causation of misfortune is a prime preoccupation in Nigerian African metaphysics.[65] Hence, many Africans have recourse to magic and divination in order to gain power from the benevolent spirits to protect them from the unseen evil forces. It should not be surprising, then, that what was branded a "spirit movement" in 1938 was only a yearning for the power of God through the Holy Spirit to permeate the practicality of the new Adventist faith. The converts who experienced the charismatic renewal understood the Adventist theory of spiritual gifts in their

---

63. Tikili, "Experiences and Convictions," 1.
64. Tikili, "Experiences and Convictions," 1–2.
65. Ilogu, "Christianity and Ibo Traditional Religion."

own context by tapping into the power of the Holy Spirit. As a result, they were able to see visions (the unseen), had power to heal, and had power to overcome evil forces.

However, this vision was not shared by the mission leaders who possibly did not fully understand the Nigerian metaphysics and the lived realties of indigenous life. Aside from branding the renewal as "ungodly," they discouraged extemporal and vibrant worship interspersed with what was perceived as noisy clapping, singing, and dancing. With less support from the church leadership on this matter, Tikili eventually resigned and established his own Church (Seventh-day Church of God), taking with him a number of followers.[66] The resignation of Tikili should not be a surprise considering his African traditional background. He must have seen the manifestation of the Spirit as part of indigenizing or localizing Adventism and making it culturally relevant.

Understandably, the Adventist leaders were wary and highly suspicious of such manifestations since it was becoming rampant among other Christian bodies. For instance, in 1930, just after the rise of Joseph Ayo Babalola, the foremost leader of Aladura Churches in Nigeria, other indigenous movements of this kind began springing up. Especially among members of the Faith Tabernacle Church in Ibadan, West of Nigeria, a prophet emerged. The name of this prophet is not mentioned in the report of W. G. Till. Till, an Adventist missionary leader, described the activities of the new leader-prophet and his followers as signs of the end time. It is likely that this was Daniel Orekoya, the healing prophet of the Oke-Bola revival in 1930, who laid the foundation of the indigenous Christ Apostolic Church, an Aladura (charismatic) movement. Till's report through the denomination's flagship magazine, *The Review*, branded the leader as a false prophet. Accordingly,

---

66. Izima, *Brief History*, 23–24. This resignation may have been around the end of 1939 or early in the 1940s, for Tikili is pictured with other Adventist workers in the June 1939 edition of *Advent Survey*. Bartlett, "United Missions Council"; interview with Solomon O. Agharaumuna, August 2019. Agharaumuna was generally considered the oldest living Adventist in Aba. See also "Bible Sabbath Association Organizational Profile."

when some inquirers came, they, the Adventist leaders, were able to point out that

> there are false prophets as well as true, and the Bible teaches that in the last days Satan will work miracles. This surprised many, and they have asked how they can differentiate, and so we have been given opportunity to witness for the truth.[67]

The opportunity to witness for the truth was a needed ingredient for the end times. Notwithstanding issues of doctrine and the end-time mantra, Till was unhappy with the charismatic style of worship practiced by the prophets and their followers. He complained that there was little preaching among the new indigenous Christians. Instead, there was much "so-called singing and chanting, interspersed freely with the clanging of a bell."[68]

Interestingly, the "spirit movement" among Adventists at the end of the 1930s also coincided with other indigenous revivals and schisms that occurred in the Apostolic Church, Assemblies of God Church, as well as other mission churches in Igboland and in Nigeria. It seems to have been a time of disagreements and disavowal of orthodoxy and orthopraxis between foreign Christian leaders and local Christian leaders[69] that led to innovation and invention of new ecclesial traditions with roots in the culture of the people of Nigeria. It was a contextual sign that Christianity in Nigeria was becoming culturally rooted and this could have been taken seriously by the Adventist missionaries instead of their response of denial and replacement. Such disagreements in opinions, theology, and praxis led to a schism which might have been avoided by Adventists through dialogue and patient cultivation of a positive view of their host cultures.

---

67. Till, "Advance on the Nigerian Front."
68. Till, "Advance on the Nigerian Front."
69. Burgess, *Nigeria's Christian Revolution*, 68–72.

SUMMARY AND CONCLUSIONS

Nigeria, a multifaceted milieu with its immense cultural diversity, welcomed Adventist missionaries as latecomers to its religious scene. Generally, institutional organizations became the avenue for maintaining the Adventist mission in Nigeria. However, after establishing their mission in Nigeria, Adventist missionaries were faced with the challenges and task of maintaining what they had started. By exploring how Adventist missionaries encountered three cultural issues and practices in Nigeria, this chapter established that Adventist missionaries consciously or unconsciously sought avenues to replace elements of traditional culture, misunderstood the value of cultural practices, exhibited impatience towards the status of their converts, and often held negative views of their host cultures. Aside from providing a substitute religio-cultural system that eventually became a subculture for converts to Adventism, any cultural practice that seemingly conflicted with the vision of a coming kingdom was discouraged. By implication, Adventist missionaries in Nigeria seemed to envision a "triumphalist" attitude to culture. This attitude sought cultural disengagement or the conquest of the cultural elements through Adventist ethos and ecclesial praxis.[70]

Nonetheless, it must be maintained that Adventist missionaries contributed in positive ways to Nigeria. This is evident especially in the educational and health facilities which contributed to a holistic view of humanity. However, the triumphalist engagement of missionaries with the indigenous culture as was demonstrated in this chapter bears significance for the historiography of Adventist mission in Nigeria.

The treatment and role of women seems to be an underexplored theme. While Adventist mission history does not undervalue the contribution of women to its history, the perception and engagement of Adventist missionaries with women in the host cultures has not been given adequate significance.

---

70. Langer, "Kingdom Integration," 30.

Secondly, when it comes to polygamy, Adventist missionaries in Nigeria not only demonized the practice, but they also destabilized families which in some ways brought disrespect to individual converts. The issue of polygamy has been explored by Höschele in the East African encounter with Adventism. Some questions remain: Were there Adventist missionaries who did not openly support the practice but condoned it for the sake of the mission or the converts?

Thirdly, the case of indigenous charismatic renewal which missionaries characterized as counterfeit may not be too surprising in the overall treatment of Adventist mission historiography. What may be interesting is if charismatic influences were ever seen in a positive light by Adventist missionaries. Moreover, since the case presented in this chapter led to a split, exploring the perspective of those who left may bring a richer perspective in exploring the dynamics of end-time rhetoric claimed by those who learned from Adventist missionaries but added more layers of discussion to the eschatological vision of the world.

Finally, the historical analysis attempted here is not just a departure from institutional mission approaches which are incapable of taking into account the complex interaction between missionaries and various local elements. It is a departure from a Eurocentric or American-centric avowal that sees everything done by missionaries as noble. It is an example of a critical engagement of mission history that attempts to grasp the unique instances and dynamics of Adventism's crossing of social, cultural, philosophical, and linguistic barriers. It is an attempt that should be encouraged in doing Adventist mission history.

Chapter 5

Independence, Civil War, and the Beginnings of Indigenization of Adventism in Nigeria from the 1940s to 1990s

THIS PENULTIMATE CHAPTER[1] PROBLEMATIZES how Adventism in Nigeria thrived from the 1940s to the late 1980s. It will be demonstrated that Nigerian Adventism began its religious independence from Western Adventism gradually. This was partly due to the unwillingness of the local Adventist workers who were seemingly comfortable with foreign leadership. In the Civil War years, Igbo Adventists who succumbed to the atrocities of the war bore a mark, in that the growth of Adventism in the Southeast of Nigeria was significantly decimated. Additionally, the campus revivals of the 1970s and 1980s marked a significant advancement in the indigenization process that had been underway prior to the Civil

---

1. Originally published as "Independence, Civil War, and the Beginnings of Indigenization of Seventh-day Adventism in Nigeria from the 1940s to 1990s," *Spes Christiana* 34 (2023) 91–116.

THE BEGINNINGS OF INDIGENIZATION

War. Due to the conflict over the question of whether to practice Christianity like Pentecostals in Nigeria or missionary Adventists, Nigerian Adventism became entangled in conversations important to the larger Christian culture.

The last chapter traced the history of Adventism in Nigeria from the 1900s to 1940s, with reference to three crucial cultural issues: the position of women in society, polygamy, and charismatic tendencies in worship. It explored the complicated and multifaceted relationships of Adventist missionaries with indigenous issues during their mission work in Nigeria. The chapter made the case that, despite their success, the missionaries' approach to Nigerian culture was tainted by issues of contention and the stark contrast of the host culture to their conception of Christ's parousia. Thus, to prepare people for Christ's second coming, all cultural practices that appeared to divert the attention of converts from the approaching supernatural kingdom had to be abandoned.

While this present chapter builds on the last, it focuses on a different route and time frame in a bid to problematize how Adventism thrived from the 1940s to the late 1980s. Three case studies will address developments which arose during those years: the political independence of Nigeria, which was realized in 1960; the Nigerian Civil War from 1967 to 1970; and the campus revivals of the 1970s and 1980s (and the departure of Western leadership) which gave rise to indigenization of Adventism in Nigeria.

These three areas are indispensable for dealing with the overall history of Nigeria and Christian mission history as well. Their relationship with the progress and advance of mission in the history of Nigeria have been documented by Richard Burgess and especially Ayodeji Abodunde, who has written the most comprehensive account of the history of Christianity in Nigeria.[2] Other scholars like Adrian Hastings, Elizabeth Isichei, and John Baur have dealt with the intricate nature of Christian mission advance in sub-Saharan Africa.[3] However, the themes have not formed a proper academic

---

2. Burgess, *Nigeria's Christian Revolution*; Abodunde, *Heritage of Faith*.

3. Hastings, *Church in Africa*; Isichei, *History of Christianity*; Baur, *2000 Years of Christianity*.

discourse in Adventist mission history in Nigeria. Either they are mentioned in passing or left out completely.[4] One exception is that of the quest for indigenous leadership in Nigeria, which was the crux of Abraham Kuranga's dissertation.[5] An important subject, the Civil War years, remains an unexplored theme in the mission history of Adventism in Nigeria. Moreover, linking the campus revivals of the 1970s and 1980s with indigenization of Adventism is a new endeavor. As this chapter will show, the three themes are intertwined in the quest to understand Adventism in Nigeria, as well as its quest for localization or indigenization.

In asking how Adventists dealt with the rise of nationalism in the mid-1940s, I will be highlighting the course Adventism in Nigeria took following political independence and the eventual independence from Western leadership. For the Civil War years, focus will be on the devastation of the War on Adventism's most successful region, Southeast Nigeria. Due to lack of historical material, I have in a few instances relied on oral interviews. Lastly, the longest section of this chapter, the campus revivals, will give attention to the student movement activities of Adventists in Nigeria. It also highlights the beginning of the quest for grounding Adventism in Nigeria.

INDEPENDENCE

In the 1940s and 1950s, Christian mission in Africa was still a flourishing project. In fact, as Isichei notes, there was a proliferation of missionary societies in this period.[6] This was particularly true for Adventists. In Nigeria, Adventist missionary activities saw a tremendous growth. In the 1950s, as Adventism continued to spread in the country, missionaries placed more emphasis on knowledge acquisition. Traces of this can be seen as far back as the late 1920s, when Adventist missionaries preoccupied themselves

---

4. See, for instance, Agboola, *Seventh-day Adventists*; Alalad, *Limiting Factors*; Alao, *90 Years*; Maigadi, *Adventist Church*.

5. Kuranga, "Seventh-day Adventism."

6. Isichei, *History of Christianity*, 325.

with establishing schools.[7] Already in 1947, the Teacher Training School at Ibadan was transferred to the Southeast and established in Ihie; it was renamed as the Nigerian Training College. In 1952, an Adventist Training College began offering classes in Otun. 1953 saw the establishment of an Adventist High School, Ihie,[8] and in 1959 the Adventist College of West Africa was founded in Ilishan-Remo, in the West of Nigeria. The college constituted the only church-run institution of higher learning for all of Nigeria and West Africa.

Although Christian mission flourished in the 1950s, the period also saw a rise in nationalist movements across the continent. In Nigeria in particular, nationalist movements grew strong from the mid-1940s up to the late 1950s, challenging and rejecting colonialism. For the nationalists, emphasis was placed on the handover of political power to Nigerians. In 1960, when Nigeria got its independence from the British Empire, the anticipated event had been spearheaded by pan-Africanist and nationalist movements that called for political and socioeconomic freedom from the tentacles of the White colonial masters.

Christian missions were not left out of this drive. Several vocal converts to Christianity followed the road traveled by nationalists. They became radical and demanded training and greater participation in the running of the missions. Such voices were largely considered dissenters due to their radical characteristics. Those voices expressed the frustrations of many nationalists who felt that "the process of indigenization was too slow, either by not giving adequate training to the nationals, or not giving them a greater part to play in the running of the missions."[9]

Thus, in the 1950s, the voices of more Nigerian Christians became outspoken in calling for independence of leadership from the foreign missionaries. This was not surprising. As a matter of interest, the educated elite who called for political and socioeconomic freedom for Nigeria were themselves trained by the

7. Kuranga, "Seventh-day Adventism," 62.
8. Izima, *Brief History*, 43.
9. Galadima and Turaki, "Christianity in Nigeria," 185.

Christian missions. Isichei has argued that the near monopoly of education by Christian missions before independence meant that the new leaders who emerged came from Christian backgrounds.[10] Personalities like Herbert Marcauley, Nnamdi Azikiwe, Obafemi Awolowo, Anthony Enahoro, and others were former students of Christian primary or secondary schools. Hence, some see the indirect contributions of Christian missions towards the attainment of Nigeria's independence. Perhaps it was the missionary teaching of the equality of all people that challenged these nationalists to question the dominance of foreigners in their nation.[11]

Nigerian Christians who saw the attainment of independence also wanted the displacement of White dominance in the leadership affairs of the Christian churches. In several ways, the call for the withdrawal of missionaries did not begin in the 1960s. It began with the various schisms, indigenous Christian movements, and breakaways starting from 1888, when the Native Baptist Church was formed. It intensified in the 1920s and 1930s and through the 1940s. How did Nigerian Adventists engage with this matter?

By the 1960s, Nigerian Adventists began calls for independence from missionary Adventism. For instance, in the West of Nigeria, several young members of the denomination felt it was time for a national leadership. According to Kuranga, those who called for religious independence were mostly laymen who were employed by the Nigerian government. Unlike other Christian bodies, where the indigenous pastors played key roles in destabilizing missionary dominance, the national Adventist pastors were inactive in this respect. For obvious reasons, they could not commit "religious treason": Their source of livelihood depended on the missionaries.[12]

It is probable that the indigenous Adventist workers were not entirely convinced of the need for an indigenous Adventist Church in Nigeria. As I will show, the move to seek religious independence

---

10. Isichei, *History of Christianity*, 339.

11. Diara and Nche, "European and American Christian Missions," 89–99; Nwadialor, "Christian Missionary Enterprise."

12. Kuranga, "Seventh-day Adventism," 136–39.

came mostly from laypeople. Thus, there is some contrast between what happened in other churches in Nigeria and the Adventist denomination. In fact, at the height for the call for political freedom by the educated elites and nationalists, Robert O. Wosu, an influential indigenous Adventist pastor, encouraged the loyalty of fellow workers to the authorities, whether foreign or indigenous, since God had given them power. The speech was delivered in December 1950 to the year-end workers' meeting in the North of Nigeria and reproduced in *The West African Advent Messenger*, an organ of the denomination. Interestingly, the speech was made after the superintendent, J. Ashford Hyde, had asked Wosu to speak on the subject. Wosu began:

> During a series of meetings of workers in the North Nigerian Mission, held December ending 1950, the superintendent Dr. J. A. Hyde asked me to speak on the above subject. As we all felt that in view of the nation-wide political mania and political freedom movement that is absorbing the interests of the masses of the people in the whole of West Africa, the superintendent has instructed me to reproduce the same message for the use and guidance of our native workers in other mission fields.[13]

Wosu encouraged workers by stating that

> we should pay taxes to the government; we must pray on behalf of rulers and obey them in all things that are not conflicting with the requirements of God. But we are not to take part in politics. We should not even express our views on the matter. Any worker who takes part in politics or even in conversation reveals his preferences or prejudices, must of necessity favour one party against another, and in that way limit his influence with the people and endanger the cause of the truth he represents.[14]

Wosu concluded that

---

13. Wosu, "Our Relation to Political Organizations."
14. Wosu, "Our Relation to Political Organizations."

> God in His Word has told us the part that the governments of this world will play in persecuting the Commandment-keeping people of God and forcing upon them the observance of Sunday, the counterfeit Sabbath, on pain of economic and social boycott, confiscation of properties, prison and finally decree their death. To vote anybody into office then is to be a partaker of his sin. We are to be good citizens, loyal subjects. We are to be good mixers and yet not get mixed up with the world.[15]

The above account is the only available written text of the period on how Adventists should relate to political matters and issues touching on political freedom or independence. What makes this text very interesting is that it came from a local worker. At face value it seems that the Adventist missionary desire to disengage converts from this world, as already argued, was successful by this time. In this vein, Wosu warned his fellow converts not to turn their attention away from the imminence of the otherworldly kingdom. Wosu seems to have been reflecting a kind of pessimist premillennialism,[16] which pioneer missionary to Nigeria, Jesse Clifford, also exhibited in dealing with issues related to politics, culture, and society.[17]

There is a possibility that Wosu was asked to speak on the matter to suppress any protest and calls for independence from Adventist missionaries. However, this possibility cannot be further pursued because of lack of historical data. In addition, the utter silence on the matter by both missionary administrators and local pastors indicates that it might not have been so important after all. On the other hand, since this speech came from an influential local worker, it is possible that the local pastors and workers were comfortable with the missionary leadership, or so it seems. Presumably, this was so since their livelihoods were tied to denominational employment.

---

15. Wosu, "Our Relation to Political Organizations."
16. Langer, "Kingdom Integration," 21–39.
17. Wogu, "Preparing Converts," 94.

THE BEGINNINGS OF INDIGENIZATION

In contrast, Adventist laypeople had an advantage over the local pastors and workers. They were not employed by the missionaries and were financially independent. According to Kuranga, most of the protests came from laypersons who had employment elsewhere.[18] At the same time, there were teachers in the denomination's schools like T. K. Popoola and J. A. Atejioye who felt it was their duty to be the mouthpiece of employed ministers. Together, these two parties were convinced of the need for indigenous leadership. They, comprising many lay youths, wrote what would be referred to today as an open letter to the West African Union. They requested that "it was time for Nigerians, by the Divine Power to take their rightful place in the Mission field."[19] Although they were not opposed to having assistance from missionaries, they felt that they could no "longer afford to fold their arms" while dancing to the tune of the White missionaries.[20]

According to the letter, if the committee which had convened at Accra for election of church leadership refused to appoint a Nigerian president, they would attribute that "to nothing but lack of confidence in ourselves."[21] The result of this kind of religious independent thinking and resistance saw the election of Joseph Adeyemo Adeogun as acting president in place of G. L. Elmstrom in 1961, and from 1962 onwards, Adeogun became president of the denomination in Western Nigeria. Already, this course of independence had happened naturally in the Southeast where Adventism grew rapidly. For instance, Albert J. Dickay, who had been serving as associate president of the East Nigerian Mission in the Southeast since the beginning of the 1950s, was made president in 1958. Dickay was the first West African to be made a president of a local mission in the region.[22] In the North of Nigeria, such progress was slower.

18. Kuranga, "Seventh-day Adventism in Western Nigeria," 136–39.
19. Letter to the West African Union of SDA Church at Accra through Pastor G.M. Elmstrom: "Inevitable Appeal," 137.
20. Letter through Pastor Elmstrom: "Inevitable Appeal," 137.
21. Letter through Pastor Elmstrom: "Inevitable Appeal," 137.
22. Coon, "General Conference Radio Secretary."

The true separation, or independence, from Western Adventism occurred between 1969 and 1980. This development has been carefully documented by David Trim, the Adventist historian and director of Archives, Statistics, and Research at the General Conference, in *A Passion for Mission*.[23] According to Trim, the "goodbye," that is, the separation from sub-Saharan Africa, was a painful episode for the Northern European Division (NED), which at the time served as the parent division overseeing missions in Nigeria as well as other African countries. Trim's archival research masterfully traces how the NED became the Northern Europe–West Africa Division (NEWAD) in 1970, following the reorganization of African territories into other divisions. He also highlights the role of both the General Conference and the NED in supporting the emergence of indigenous leadership within African churches.[24] Of special interest, Trim discusses the denunciation of prejudice towards Africans (and "Blacks") at a General Conference Session, along with the desire of then General Conference President Robert H. Pierson to see the Adventist Church in Africa become "authentically African."[25] While I do not engage that dimension here, since my focus lies primarily on the internal dynamics of Nigerian Adventism in its pursuit of independence, I believe Trim's perspective is worth considering.

CIVIL WAR

As the bells of independence kept tolling for the young nation Nigeria, tragedy soon struck. The country was hit by a civil war in 1967. It was a catastrophe that not only destabilized the dreams of those who basked in the sunshine of a new era, but those of the Christian denominations as well. When Nigeria got its independence in 1960, nearly everyone recognized that Nigeria was an extremely diverse place, geographically, politically, economically,

23. Trim, *Passion for Mission*, ch. 7.
24. Trim, *Passion for Mission*, 167–87.
25. Trim, *Passion for Mission*, 174–75.

and culturally. It is interesting to read again the words of Hugh Clifford, governor general of Nigeria (1919–25), who earlier dismissed the idea of Nigeria as a nation because of intersectional and complex differences. But as the new country celebrated in the euphoria of independence, the multiple levels of divisions began showing their ugly heads. Inability to achieve regionalism and ethnic diversity constituted two major problems that barred the development of a national identity.[26] Regionalism could not be achieved because of the multiple ethnic groups in Nigeria. Ethnic bigotry played major roles in the years that led to the Civil War. After the collapse of the democratic system in 1963, there were ferocious confrontations in the 1964/1965 elections. This led to the growth of ethnic and regional antagonisms.

The optimism that had existed a few years earlier had now given way to disillusionment. As the country seemed to have lost hope in the elections, in 1966 a military coup was carried out followed by a countercoup that brought General Yakubu Gowon to power. In the North of Nigeria, a series of well-targeted violent actions was directed towards the Igbos, forcing them to return to their homelands. Soon there was a formal secession and declaration of the "Republic of Biafra" by Colonel Odumegwu Ojukwu, the military governor of the Eastern region. While the Biafrans argued that they were forced out of the federation, the federal government of Nigeria viewed the declaration as an act of rebellion. Hence the Civil War erupted, lasting three years with an estimated three million Igbo casualties.[27]

The Civil War had ominous implications:

> The combination of social dislocation, growing fatalities, lack of food and medical facilities, air raids and the threat of genocide created a series of individual and social crises that precipitated profound changes in the Igbo religious landscape.[28]

26. Falola and Heaton, *History of Nigeria*, 156.
27. Falola, *Violence in Nigeria*, 1; Burgess, *Nigeria's Christian Revolution*, 36–37.
28. Burgess, *Nigeria's Christian Revolution*, 37.

As Igbo society disintegrated, with many becoming refugees and living with the resulting insecurities, several Igbos began looking for alternatives for a better life, *ezindu*. Religious revival became an inevitable outcome. Burgess has argued that the Biafran crisis not only exposed the deficiencies of the existing religious options for Igbos; it created a favorable environment for a religious revival which flourished because it adapted successfully to new and challenging contexts by re-sacralizing the landscape of Christianity, "bringing renewal to existing churches, generating new theological emphases 'from below,' and precipitating fresh mission initiatives."[29] Burgess further affirmed that "many Igbos found the dominant brand of Christianity, represented by mainline churches, lacked power to help them fulfil their deep-seated aspirations, cope with the stresses engendered by the War, and engage effectively in mission."[30] As a result, they were drawn to "born-again" Christianity and Pentecostalism, both of which emphasized the power of transformation and a "reliance on direct experience of the divine," affirming spiritual realities and promising power for healing and deliverance.[31]

While Burgess' argument holds for many mainline Igbo Christians, the story of Igbo Adventists was different. The Adventists who were in the Southeast when the war broke out held on to their apocalyptic faith and doctrines, the strings that formed their subculture. This was not surprising since Adventists were in the minority as compared to other mainline churches. But as the war progressed, the stories of faith began changing. While Adventists in the rest of the country went to church freely, lived and had access to basic social amenities, many young male Igbo Adventists with their Christian counterparts were conscripted into the Biafran army. Other young men who escaped conscription hid in holes in the ground or lived in the forest and jungle to evade conscription. Many who were not conscripted voluntarily joined the Biafran army. I asked a close relative, an Adventist, why he joined the army

---

29. Burgess, *Nigeria's Christian Revolution*, 37.
30. Burgess, *Nigeria's Christian Revolution*, 37.
31. Burgess, *Nigeria's Christian Revolution*, 37.

even though Adventists were known to be pacifists. To him, it was for self-defense and to protect their newly founded country. In his words, "In a situation where Igbos were going to be annihilated, a reasonable Igbo man will tend to defend himself. If you tell anyone who reads the Bible, who also studied history, the person will tend to defend himself."[32] When I asked if he was not concerned that Adventists were on the other side of the line, he responded: "It was not an Adventist war, it was a political ethnic war; we were not fighting a religious war, but a war of survival of our race."[33]

Institutionally, the Adventist organization in the Southeast began losing its properties. As soon as Aba fell in September 1968, the administrative headquarters began moving from one location to another (Umuocha, Ihie, Amaum ara in Mbaise, and Umueze in Mbano).[34] At the same time, the consequences of war—poverty, hunger, and starvation—became the norm. In the wake of the war, Adventists outside Nigeria began sending supply relief in a coordinated fashion. In addition to setting aside special worship days to collect offerings, relief teams were set up in collaboration with the denomination's Adventist Welfare Service and Red Cross to send aid for war victims. Supplies included clothes, vitamin pills, medical items, baby food, milk, and stockfish.[35] While the denomination's relief agency came to the aid of Biafran Adventists, as did CARITAS, many Adventist churches and the denomination's hospitals served as refugee settlements.

While several missionaries withdrew as the war escalated, a few medical missionaries stayed until the end of the war. Mention should be made of Dr. Sherman A. Nagel Jr., the administrator of the Adventist-owned hospital in Okpualangwa near Aba. Nagel made sure the health facility functioned for most of the Civil War. And when Okpualangwa was taken by the federal troops in

32. Interview with a former Biafran soldier, name withheld, 2020.

33. Interview with a former Biafran soldier, name withheld, 2020.

34. Njoku, "History of Seventh-day Adventist Church," 61; cf. Izima, *Brief History*, 33–34.

35. See "News from All Over"; Turner, "Put Biafra in Your Prayers"; Wilson, "What Is It Like."

December 1969, the health facility was transferred to Emii, Owerri, where it continued its humanitarian services.[36]

The role of the Adventist denomination in providing humanitarian and relief services where needed did not stop many Adventists from succumbing to the realities of war. Moreover, relief could not reach everyone. As a result of starvation and kwashiorkor, Adventists who were known for their strict dietary rules also joined others in eating all kinds of things including rats, lizards, dogs, etc., for survival. According to an interviewee, at first Adventists did not partake in eating all kinds of meat because of their strict dietary laws.[37] However, with pangs of hunger, Igbo Adventists joined "their fellow humans" in eating anything out of desperation to stay alive. There are war stories from young Adventist Biafran soldiers who witnessed this.[38] There are also stories of Adventist members who tried to eat their pastor because he was a foreigner![39] From these stories, it could be said that even though Igbo Adventists retained their faith, the Adventist apocalyptic message of hope and God's willingness to provide for them as the remnant did not play a strong role at the time when it was needed most. Moreover, ethnic prejudice had sunk deep into the lives of the Igbos, who were being slaughtered daily.

It should not be surprising that in times of war the true nature of humanity is revealed. This includes Adventists, who claimed to be the agents and catalysts of God's kingdom by separating from the world while waiting for the parousia through true worship of God. At the danger of sounding excessively evaluative at this point, having reflected on the above, it may not be out of place to

---

36. Izima, *Brief History*, 33–34; Wilson, "What Is It Like," 11–12. See full coverage from the perspective of an American doctor in Krum, "Directed by God's Providence."

37. Telephone interview with Dr. Emmanuel Oriaku, 2020.

38. My father was a Biafran soldier who was conscripted as a Biafran soldier directly from the Adventist secondary school, Ihie. He told me of his experiences during the war. Due to the gory nature of those experiences, I will not go into further details.

39. On the story of church members attempting to eat their own pastor, see Bauman, *African Safari for Jesus*, 108–11.

ask if the role of missionary Adventism was to make individuals more Adventist than Christian. By the end of the Nigerian Civil War in January 1970, Adventists had lost their property, buildings, schools, and hospitals in the Southeast. In the subsequent months, the few institutions owned by the denomination were nationalized by the military government. As a result, the church was left with no institution in the region where it had had most of its success.[40]

While the denomination grew and prospered in the West and North, Adventists in the South, and especially the Southeast, began rebuilding, reconnecting, and restructuring after the Biafran War. One way to achieve this was through numerous evangelistic meetings held by local pastors and evangelists.[41] The evangelistic meetings served as recourse to explain the end of the times which had come upon the Igbos especially. Another step towards rebuilding was the celebration, at the beginning of 1973, of the golden jubilee of the arrival of Adventism in the South of Nigeria.[42] The celebration served to revel in the success of the denomination in that region, despite its most recent setbacks. That same year, the push for the creation of a body that governed the denomination in Nigeria led to the establishment of Nigeria Union Mission, which was created out of the West African Union Mission.[43] Although its president and secretary were Scandinavian missionaries (Sievert Gustavsson and P. R. Lindstrom), the local administrative units were mostly headed by Nigerians.

CAMPUS REVIVALS AND THE MOVE TOWARDS INDIGENIZING ADVENTISM

Seemingly, it was the local leadership that encouraged a major campus revival that brewed among Adventist students and young

---

40. Eva, "Ahoada Hospital in Nigeria."
41. Chucks, "New Branch Sabbath School."
42. Agboola, "Golden Jubilee," 12.
43. Agboola, Golden Jubilee," 12.

people in the late 1970s and early 1980s. The early 1980s campus revival arose from three noteworthy factors explored below.

The first factor that precipitated the revival is closely related to the introduction of all-night prayer services to Adventist circles. This ritual, where believers gathered to pray throughout the night, was a new venture among Adventists and it attracted young people, especially those students on the public university campuses who had seen the practice in other churches. In April 1969, after a Sabbath service, Adventist students at the University of Ibadan formed a union known as the "Adventist Students' Union." It was attended and conducted by the Union and local Mission officers since it was a milestone among Adventists in Nigeria.[44] Soon, other chapters of the Adventist Students' Union began forming at other universities and places of higher education, including the denominationally owned Adventist College of West Africa, ACWA.[45]

By the end of the 1970s, there were several Adventist Students' Unions on public campuses and universities. By the beginning of the 1980s, the Unions morphed into local Adventist Student Fellowships (ASF) under the National Association of Adventist Students (NAAS). Soon, several members of the local ASFs began attending an all-night prayer service at Oke-Bola in Ibadan, the headquarters of the denomination in Western Nigeria.[46] Interestingly, all-night prayer services among Adventists were not new. In fact, they had been started by Pastor A. F. Oloyede in Abeokuta in 1972 for the purpose of praying and studying the Bible with Adventists and non-Adventists; they were then called "Night of Prayer."[47] The practice must have been accepted and copied in other churches since it was conducted on Sabbath every first Friday of the month. However, the reason why Adventist students trooped to Oke-Bola was different.

44. Babatunde, "Adventists at the University of Ibadan."

45. See, e.g., the report about the inauguration of the Union at the University of Ife in December 1969, in Kolade, "Light Shines."

46. Babalola, "Assessment of the Impact," 78.

47. Ukegbu, "Blessedness of Communion with God."

THE BEGINNINGS OF INDIGENIZATION

Early in 1980/1981, a young Adventist, Onolapo Ajibade, who had just returned from Ghana after completing a Bachelor of Science in Agriculture, decided to become a literature evangelist for the Adventist denomination in Ibadan. As a new convert who had read Ellen White's *Great Controversy*, his passion to spread his newfound faith led him to decide to make a living by selling Adventist books to the public. According to Ajibade, this decision spurred a kind of enthusiasm and zeal among young Adventists at public universities for lay evangelism. The young Adventists would meet once a month on a particular weekend in Oke-Bola, the conference headquarters in Ibadan, where they prayed and planned for outreach. The meetings were led by Ajibade. According to him, "we did all night not because we wanted it, but because it was the most convenient."[48] They had planned to meet on Friday and end their meetings on Sunday. However, since most of the participants were students who did not bring food along (some only brought biscuits for the whole weekend), it was not practical to meet regularly. Therefore,

> we decided that the only way we could meet once in a month was after Sabbath service. People could travel from the universities and environs to Oke-Bola and we would pray all night on Saturday . . . and dispersed on Sunday morning. That became our regular means of meeting together.[49]

The second factor leading to the revival was the dissatisfaction of second-generation Adventists with the formalism of worship and spirituality in Adventist circles. According to Israel B. Olaore, who became a leader of the students around 1982, young Adventists were no longer satisfied with the reserved spirituality and the rationalistic mode of worship that they were used to. The students felt that they knew a lot of doctrinal teachings but were not connected to God and could not express this in worship. In Olaore's words:

---

48. Interview with Onolapo Ajibade, 2020.
49. Interview with Onolapo Ajibade, 2020.

> I was a cultural Adventist but not a vibrant Christian. I was not born again. A person who is not born again is just like a "cultured accent" to a body of beliefs. Being born again is an authentic expression of what the Bible calls transformation in the life of the believer. If you are not born again—you are not born-again.[50]

Moreover, Olaore was once told that the Adventist fellowship was dead after he had invited a student to attend a worship service. Hence Olaore, together with other students with a strong conviction to catalyze reformation, initiated and planned a week of revival in 1982 at the University of Ife. It is possible that the planned week of campus revival was connected to the Ajibade story and all-night prayers at Oke-Bola.

Ajibade soon became assistant publishing director of the local conference. Hence, he was seen as a beacon, a vibrant Adventist to the extent of forfeiting his university degree to work for the Lord. Ajibade's influence swiftly drew dissatisfied young Adventists who longed for more fervor in their spirituality. The result of both the all-night prayers and the 1982 week of revival was a renewed passion among Adventist students for God and ministry. A vibrant worship style of praise and worship ensued, and the use of percussion, speaking in tongues, and the born-again slogan became ways of expressing Adventist faith among those students. In fact, according to Babalola, some of those who attended the prayers at Oke-Bola also organized and initiated evangelistic outreach programs.[51]

The third factor is closely related to the fertile ground provided by local Adventist leadership for the revival. As mentioned earlier, although Adventists had employed a number of local workers, the Nigerian Union Mission leadership was headed by Scandinavians. Hence the traditional worship style of singing hymns and playing Western musical instruments, following proper liturgy, where the sermon played a major role, was upheld.

---

50. Interview with Israel B. Olaore, 2020.

51. Babalola, "Assessment of the Impact," 78. Reverberations of the early 1980s revival among Adventist students will not be treated here.

The Western musical instruments, though exotic, were foreign to Adventist converts. In fact, Kuranga concludes that when Yoruba Adventists decided to spice up worship with local instruments, the idea was not welcomed by the leadership. Because the instruments were related to non-Christian rituals, "the Adventist missionaries banned them in the Church services and substituted in their stead Western musical instruments, such as piano and organ,"[52] a move which maintained the missionaries' notions of order in worship. Olaore even concludes that the "Nordic missionaries" were afraid of expressive worship.

At the same time, David O. Babalola, the local conference president, whose territory included Oke-Bola and its environs, in his efforts to motivate the younger generation and students in the public campuses, encouraged such activities. According to Ajibade, Babalola "gave the youths the opportunity to practice their faith the way they wanted. But he made sure that we did not go against the teachings of the church."[53] Hence, Babalola encouraged Ajibade, who had become the assistant publishing director of the local conference, to lead and organize all-night prayers in Oke-Bola. Olaore concludes,

> I will say it is the combination of the support we had from the conference leadership at that time plus [the fact that] on campus we had a group of young people who wanted more than just a cultural expression that had no spiritual fervor.[54]

Lastly, and most importantly, the 1970s' intense national religious awakening among Nigerian youths and in public campus revivals must have provided a fertile ground for the Adventist revivals. Matthews Ojo has written extensively on the 1970 religious awakening in Nigeria. Before the national phenomenon in the 1970s, the research of Burgess shows that from 1967 and especially 1968 onwards, the Biafran War was a catalyst for the revivals

52. Kuranga, "Seventh-day Adventism in Western Nigeria," 205.
53. Interview with Onalapo Ajibade, 2020.
54. Interview with Israel B. Olaore, 2020.

and religious awakening among youths who were connected with the Scripture Union in war-torn Biafra.[55] Ojo has argued that the revival only became a national phenomenon after its occurrence at the University of Ibadan. As Ojo writes:

> In January 1970 revival broke out when some students in the Christian Union claimed to have been baptized in the Holy Spirit in a private prayer meeting. Though a small group, three of them who were leaders of the Christian Union, boldly shared their Pentecostal experience. Within a short time, more students accepted the experience, and it soon spread to other Christians groups such as the Student Christian Movement (established in Nigeria about 1937) and Scripture Union (established in 1887), and to other universities. In fact, by 1973, the revival was so strong that some Christian students hoisted a big banner at the gate of the then University of Ife (now Obafemi Awolowo University) with a bold inscription, "Welcome to Jesus University."[56]

As Ojo has maintained, there were social and economic factors that made the Nigerian religious context fertile for this kind of revival. The oil boom which the country experienced in the 1970s resulted in rapid economic growth. There was incremental expansion in the higher education sector. Soon the lack of accountability in public affairs and the high level of corruption in the Nigerian military-led government became apparent. This led to a wide level of social inequality and uneven development in the country. Culturally, a shift began to take place. The communalism of traditional society began to give way to hyper-individualism and an unrestrained desire for material accumulation. In the wake of the corruption that ensued in the 1970s and 1980s, the country's economic fortunes suddenly imploded. The result was a disillusioned vision among the young and relatively educated people who were concentrated in urban centers. Since the postcolonial secular state

---

55. Burgess, *Nigeria's Christian Revolution*, 2008.

56. Ojo, "Pentecostalism and Charismatic Movements in Nigeria," 80; Ojo, "Deeper Life Christian Ministry"; Ojo, "Deeper Life Bible Church in Nigeria."

had failed the young and middle-class elite, they started looking for alternative solutions. Ojo is right in his analysis that many found the solution in Pentecostal and charismatic Christianity.[57]

In the 1970s revival experience, the students at the University of Ibadan suddenly claimed the baptism of the Holy Spirit and began speaking in tongues. Despite opposition from their fellow students, the group publicized their new experience of being "born again" which soon spread even to the Student Christian Movement (SCM) group on the campus. Soon, the Christian Union established a new group, World Action Team for Christ (WATC), with the aim of spreading their born-again and Pentecostal beliefs all over Nigeria.[58] As a result, early in the 1980s, Adventist students like Olaore on public campuses caught the enthusiasm of the born-again awakening, leading to a historic revival among Adventist young people which still has its reverberations today, although it did not happen without opposition.

By 1985, the denominational leadership in Nigeria was handed over to the nationals after Helge Andersen, the last foreign president of the Nigerian Union Mission, returned to Denmark on account of ill health. Caleb O. Adeogun, the first indigenous president of the denomination in Nigeria,[59] continued in the tradition of the missionaries—he was known as "the policy man"[60] and to be eagerly concerned with upholding the integrity of church rules. He once said: "If you want to have fruitful and blessed ministry you must abide with the policies of the church, otherwise the policy will throw you out."[61]

It is not surprising that after Pastor G. Solademi, the Lay Activities and Sabbath School director at the Union under Adeogun's leadership, wrote a long letter to David Babalola encouraging the termination of the all-night prayers, the activity dwindled considerably. While James Babalola in a recent dissertation asserts that

57. Ojo, *End-Time Army*.
58. Ojo, "Charismatic Movement in Nigeria Today," 114.
59. Fly, "ASWA"; Fly, "African-Indian Ocean."
60. Adeogun Jr., "Adeogun, Caleb Oyelayo."
61. Adeogun Jr., "Adeogun, Caleb Oyelayo."

it was the administration of Adeogun that banned the activities of all-night prayer services and sessions in Adventist churches in a workers' meeting of 1988,[62] Ajibade, who was part of the local conference administration, claimed otherwise. To him, the letter from Solademi that attempted to stop the activity was not entirely welcomed by the Union. The letter expressed concern that the revival activities which centered around the all-night prayer ritual were strange to Adventism, hence they should be stopped.

However, David Babalola did not heed the directive since there was nothing wrong. Babalola, being well aware of the conflict potential in such revivalist activities, cautioned the youths not to do anything "un-Adventist."[63] Hence, the practices were not stopped by the leadership though they did dwindle over time. Ajibade claims that the main reason for the dwindling zeal was situational. The founding and core participants of the all-night prayer group soon graduated, moved to find jobs, got married and busy. Hence the zeal and time which was present in the initial cohesion of young students was no longer affordable.[64]

These two potential reasons for this decline have their merits and may not be entirely conflicting. On the one hand, the concern of Solademi may have grown out of the rumors that Adventist students were gradually adopting charismatic practices in their campus worship services. The growing influence of the Pentecostal born-again practices must have created the fear that if these were encouraged in Oke-Bola, they would spread into the local Adventist churches in the region. That a Union executive expressed such concern meant that there were others in the background who were uncomfortable with all-night prayer because it was "strange" to Adventism, as Solademi claimed. Hence, support for the activity, even from the leadership, must have dwindled. Besides, James Babalola, who wrote a dissertation on the impact of charismatic movements among Adventists, claimed to have been part of the

---

62. Babalola, "Assessment of the Impact," 79.
63. Interview with Onalapo Ajibade, 2020.
64. Interview with Onalapo Ajibade, 2020.

workers' meeting that banned the activities.⁶⁵ On the other hand, the argument regarding circumstantial factors, that students moved away, is highly substantial. Moreover, their leaders like Olaore and David Olubukola (Bukky) Ajide went abroad for further studies. Thus, the revival dwindled on the surface.

MISSIONARY ADVENTISM OR NIGERIAN ADVENTISM? AN APPRAISAL OF THE 1990S

What Ajibade did not mention was that the all-night prayers never really stopped. In fact, followers of Ajide had begun a special kind of fellowship that adopted many practices of the new and burgeoning charismatic-Pentecostal movement in Nigeria in the 1980s and 1990s. But the evidence of continuity remained hidden for some time. For, while the leaders of the general religious revival and renewal graduated and began establishing Pentecostal and charismatic churches, their Adventist counterparts graduated and largely traveled abroad for further studies. Thus, the all-night prayers seemingly went underground. After the supposed ban in 1988, the practice remained in the confines of house fellowships.

At that time, house fellowships had just become a new movement among Nigerian Christians. Enoch Adeboye of the Redeemed Christian Church of God and Folorunsho Kumuyi of the Deeper Life Ministries visited Dr. Paul Yonggi Cho of Seoul, South Korea, a strong advocate of prolonged prayer sessions and pastor of the largest Pentecostal congregation in the world during the decades that followed.⁶⁶ James Babalola, who also experienced the campus revival, claimed that he was part of those who encouraged all-night prayers at house fellowships even into the 1990s. He reports that when he was a pastor in Yaba, Lagos, the practice spread like wildfire after they rotated the night prayers among homes. According to him,

---

65. Babalola, "Assessment of the Impact," 79.
66. Waribako, *Nigerian Pentecostalism*, 31; Ojo, "Charismatic Movement," 117.

it was observed that there was a gap that was not filled by the church; the constant coming together recreated a platform for young people, especially young graduates, for fervency of spirituality. Adventist Youth Ministries had its place but there was another dimension that this fervency of worship had in this All-Night session.[67]

However, Babalola met with resistance while pastoring the Yaba Church until he also went abroad in 1993. This did not stop the practice; neither did the resistance stop in the West of Nigeria. Soon conflicts spilled over to music and instruments. For instance, when the Adventist sociologist Ronald Lawson visited Nigeria, he reported the following:

> [When I] arrived in Lagos, Nigeria, the headquarters of the Nigerian Union, I was told in my initial interview with the Union Secretary that a major issue at that time was whether or not to permit the playing of drums as part of church music. The early missionaries had banned drums because they were used in ceremonies related to the celebration of the spirits of the ancestors. However, recently the youth had pressed to change this rule because drums were integral to indigenous music. The Union had decided to allow their use under certain conditions, but when many older members complained bitterly, the church leaders had reversed their decision, and had again banned the drums. The Union Secretary added that some of the university students were attending Pentecostal services on campus because they enjoyed their music so much.[68]

This bickering tension and contestation towards this kind of renewal among Adventists grew as the years progressed. In the South, East, and North of Nigeria, this tension had not yet begun since the traditional Adventist mode of worship and liturgy was maintained. For the Igbos, the majority of Adventists, following the footsteps of missionary Jesse Clifford (or whom Igbo Adventists refer to as *Ukwu Clifford*), was what mattered as pure Adventism.

67. Babalola, "Assessment of the Impact," 80.
68. Lawson, "Sources of the Current Crisis."

In the late 1990s, Igbo Adventists constituted the major group that resisted the Pentecostal influence, in addition to the Northerners and other groups that later came to embrace missionary Adventism. The clamor for preservation was, of course, understandable: Since the Christian religious scene in Nigeria generally rushed in one direction, i.e., Pentecostalism, most Adventists in Nigeria wished to hold on to their denominational identity passed on from the missionaries. This should not be astonishing, for denominations naturally find their primary identity in their organizational self-understanding. This results in thinking of the church in functional terms where the church feels its responsibility of doing something for God in the world.[69]

In the case of the Nigerian Adventist denomination, which was and is still governed by the headquarters in the United States, the function of the denomination is to warn and prepare the world for the parousia—the end of the world and the ushering in of a new kingdom. This means separation from other churches who do not keep the Sabbath and do not worship in an orderly manner that demonstrates awe to God. Hence, mingling with other churches, and allowing practices of other churches among Adventists, allegedly amounted to a refusal of the primary role of the church, or its functional identity. Therefore, the majority of Nigerian Adventists generally embraced the notion that their role was that of a denomination that had not yet joined the Pentecostal train or "false revival."

SUMMARY AND CONCLUSION

This chapter attempted to explore the various ways Adventists and Adventism thrived during the independence era, the Civil War years, and campus revivals in Nigeria. During the independence era, it was demonstrated that Nigerian Adventism began its religious independence gradually. This was partly due to the local Adventist workers who were seemingly comfortable with foreign

69. Van Gelder, "Rethinking Denominations and Denominationalism."

leadership and their unwillingness to catalyze independent leadership. This was also in contrast to fellow Christian workers who spearheaded their religious independence. The eventual religious independence was catalyzed by lay Adventists. This in turn began the process of Adventism's localization and indigenization in Nigeria, begun from below. The Nigerian story is a clear example of indigenization or localization from below, which was quite different from other Christian mission bodies that initiated indigenization from above.

The Civil War years that devastated the progress of Adventism in the Southeast became a stain among Igbo Adventists who participated in the war and its realities. While wartime is difficult and sensitive, Igbo Adventists were truly concerned with being Adventists rather than Christians. It also shows that Adventist missionary catechesis had its limitations in Nigeria.

Lastly, the process of indigenization that started before the Civil War years made great progress in the 1970s and 1980s with the campus revivals. While Nigerian Adventism became more controlled by local leadership, Adventist ecclesial praxis began taking root in Nigerian culture. As a result, Nigerian Adventism got embroiled in the overall Christian culture, whether to worship like Pentecostals in Nigeria or to follow missionary Adventism, a tension which is still visible today. This demonstrates that Adventism in Nigeria is in a process of indigenization. It also demonstrates the healthy tension between missionary Adventism and Nigerian Adventism. This tension is healthy because it shows that Nigerian Adventists are concerned about holding on to the heritage of the missionaries while seeking relevance in their society.

Finally, while the chapter has reflected on the interaction of Adventism in Nigeria with cultural, situational, political, and religious issues in the years following the independence of Nigeria and the Civil War, the issue of indigenization was only touched on briefly. What was highlighted was the beginning of the process in the 1970s, 1980s, and 1990s. The attempt to "Pentecostalize" Adventism in Nigeria is one way some laypeople and pastors chose to respond to the discrepancies between Adventist traditions and cultural realities in Nigeria.

In this vein, Adventism in Nigeria, just like elsewhere in Africa, is caught between the vast cultural differences of African and Adventist (denominational) belief systems. This in turn generates crises of identity. While the theme of crises of identity is given more attention in the next chapter, further study of indigenous Christianity in Nigeria vis-à-vis Adventism will shed some light on this area. It will also deepen our understanding of how a premillennialist denomination, interested in the otherworldly, makes its traditions, heritage, and teachings relevant in the here and now.

Chapter 6

Nkeiruka and the Future of Adventism in Nigeria
Toward a Contextualized Mission History

ADVENTISM IN NIGERIA IS a thriving faith, a fact that mirrors the denomination's global presence. Adventism's theology and practices have undergone dynamic development in Nigeria, shaped by the country's unique history and socioreligious context. This uniqueness and dynamism are a result of the approaches of Adventist Western missionaries as well as the distinctive history and development of the Nigerian socioreligious sphere.

In this final chapter,[1] I will explore the responses of Nigerians to Adventism and how the faith has evolved in the country. The foregoing discourse will contextualize the insights made in chapters 1 to 5. Thus, in this concluding chapter, I will discuss the acceptance of Adventism in the early days when Western evangelism dichotomized faith after its acceptance. In addition, I will highlight the later tendency to Africanize the faith by adoption of Nigerian cultural elements, and the recent move toward adaptation of a

---

1. Originally published as "Nigerian Adventism: History and Promise," *Spectrum* 51 (2023) 79–88.

Pentecostal worldview. These developments have led to questions of Adventist identity if not a crisis of faith for many. Finally, I will argue for a unique Nigerian Adventism that may emerge in the future that reflects the country's unique cultural and religious context.

WESTERN ADVENTIST MISSIONARY THINKING AND THE NIGERIAN RESPONSE

Firstly, let me restate the already established fact that because of Adventism's late arrival to Nigeria there was a smaller field for doing mission since other denominational missionaries preceded Adventists. For instance, the Catholics had dominated the South and Southeast of Nigeria by 1900s, when Adventists officially established their first mission.

Be that as it may, the Adventist apocalyptic ideology of the soon return of Christ was the main preoccupation of the missionaries. To be Adventist, one needed to move outside their comfort zone and direct their energies towards the external unseen or otherworldly unseen with the hope or expectation of making it to heaven at the parousia when Christ comes.

The impending end of the world fostered a missionary zeal to warn non-Adventists and to win them as remnants. This meant converts needed to keep the Sabbath holy on Saturday, they needed to live a healthy lifestyle of eating properly according to the Levitical laws, and to abstain from alcohol, caffeine, etc. Jewelry was not accepted and proper dress prescribed. In addition, the missionaries came with their own way of transferring this ideology. They established schools, printed books, and magazines; had organizations and healthcare systems such that converts would have Bible study on Saturday; went to the Adventist school system during weekdays; visited the Adventist clinic when they were ill; and worked in the Adventist press when they needed jobs. Thus, converts were supposed to enter the Adventist world/ideology and bid farewell to their traditions, culture, friends, and in most cases their families who disagreed with them.

How did Nigerians respond to the Adventist faith? In the early days, Adventism was moderately accepted in Nigeria. However, Adventism was also perceived as a foreign religion that was not fully compatible with African (Nigerian) culture and traditions. Thus, there were tendencies to dichotomize Adventism, separating it from Nigerian culture and traditions. Some Nigerians felt that Adventism was too Western and sought to adapt it to fit their own cultural and religious practices. This led to Africanization, the attempt to make Adventism culturally relevant and multiple religious belonging, the combination of Adventism and traditional beliefs.

Acceptance of Early Adventism

The Adventist message of the imminent second coming of Jesus Christ resonated with many Nigerians, particularly those who had experienced the hardships of colonialism and the Second World War. Adventism's emphasis on healthful living and education also appealed to many Nigerians, and the denomination established several schools and healthcare institutions in the country.

The success of Adventism in Nigeria especially in its founding days was due to the acceptance of the religious ideology by some Yoruba, many Igbo, and some Hausa Nigerians. Three cases show why conversion to Adventism grew in Nigeria.

Among the Yoruba, where David C. Babcock, the first official missionary to Nigeria, first landed, the missionary's strategy was to introduce formal education, and this yielded many Yoruba conversions. In 1915–16, Babcock and his group of missionaries established a school in Sao (Shao), Ilorin, which was a breakthrough for the Adventist mission. The school grew to become the first official Adventist educational institution in Nigeria after serving the three stations of Erunmu, Sao, and Ipoti-Ekiti. In addition to reading, writing, and math, these students received extensive training in evangelism as well as in entrepreneurial skills like bricklaying, furniture making, carpentry, etc.[2] Since the locals wanted their children to have a formal education, they sent them to the Adventist school. These students later became mission employees who would serve as local evangelists and workers in bringing more Yorubas to Adventism.

More acceptance to Adventism was seen in the Southeast of Nigeria among the Igbos who were generally open to Christianity. Nevertheless, Adventism's early success in Igboland was attributed to the camp meetings that took place in 1928 and 1929. It turned out to be a successful strategy for operations in the Southeast. The camp-meeting-booth style, made of palm fronds, was appropriate for the Ngwa Igbos, who did not live in towns or cities but rather in compounds with several thatch houses nearby. The camp meetings were a novelty in that region, and as a result, Adventists drew lots of Igbos who just attended the events to see what was going on. At the same time, the preaching and Bible studies held during those camp meetings led to many conversions.

In the North of Nigeria, it was medical mission that brought a breakthrough. When John and Louisa Hyde went to the North of Nigeria in the early 1930s, they met with serious resistance. Muslims predominated in the Jengre region, which made mission challenging. Since Mrs. Hyde was a licensed nurse, the Hydes opened a dispensary. The dispensary, which subsequently evolved into the Jengre SDA Hospital, gave access to those in the Jengre neighborhood who were in urgent need of medical care. One instance was Louisa Hyde's therapy for the jigger flea. She removed the parasite from the patients' soles. The people in the area were drawn to Adventism such that a group of about fifty chiefs once came to the Hydes during a visit by William McClements, superintendent of the mission in Nigeria, to learn more about the Adventist medical work. These traditionalists stated that Adventism was needed in their region.[3]

---

2. Agboola, *Seventh-day Adventist History*, 26.
3. See Wogu, "Trailblazers."

Multiple Religious Belonging in the Face of Dichotomization

Multiple religious belonging already was an issue before the coming of Adventists. For instance, Rosalind Hackett notes the ubiquity of people in Calabar, Nigeria, who belonged to several Christian and non-Christian religious groups simultaneously.[4] Adventist missionaries were suspicious of these kinds of multiple allegiances, so they almost always refused such groups of people who wanted to join their movement. For instance, when Jesse Clifford, an Adventist missionary, encountered a group of indigenous Sabbatarians in the Niger Delta, he was faced with the dilemma of whether to adopt this group of Sabbatarians as foundational members of the local Adventist church. Jesse Clifford decided not to since most of the Sabbatarians were polygamists and engaged in other strange practices and customs. Incorporating this group into the Adventist body would have entailed no radical break with the past and the difficulty of policing/enforcing Adventist ideology.

Interestingly, many converts from traditional religion among Igbos and Yorubas joined Adventism. But the issue was that Adventist missionaries must have made a mistake to think of conversion in a monolithic rather than a dynamic sense in Nigeria. Due to this monolithic thinking of conversion, missionaries dichotomized Adventism, separating it from Nigerian culture and traditions. Adventism had to exist (in a vacuum) in Nigeria, outside of the influence of indigenous culture and tradition which was termed pagan and evil. Thus, while Adventism brought intellectual, social, and health development for many, for others, it did not speak to their lived realities.

Since Western Adventism did not speak to the psyche of Nigerians, converts would visit native doctors and juju priests when a problem which could not be handled medically or intellectually arose. This led to the emergence of a unique form of Adventism in Nigeria that combined elements of both Adventism and traditional African religion. For example, some Nigerian Adventists

---

4. Hackett, *Religion in Calabar*.

incorporated elements of ancestor worship and divination into their religious practices, while others adapted Adventist teachings to fit their beliefs in reincarnation and spirit possession.

Africanization of Adventism

Africanization here means the process of giving Adventism an African identity, and in the case of our discussion, a Nigerian identity. In the analysis between Christian missionaries and indigenous peoples, conversion, according to David Lindenfeld, could suggest a change in sensibility that occurs within an individual; for others, it suggests a group process that can have dramatic social consequences. As Lindenfield further posits, "It does not take long for missionaries to lose control of the message once the Bible is in the hands of the indigenes."[5] It seems this was the main fear of the missionaries.

For instance, in the 1930s in Aba, after a charismatic renewal among Adventist converts, Adventist missionaries branded the revival as Spiritism. The revival among Adventist converts came after they studied the gifts of the Holy Spirit. It saw several members claiming the power of the Spirit to see visions and dreams, heal the sick, raise the dead, make the lame to walk, etc. While others prophesied and spoke in tongues, others openly confessed their sins and were flogged publicly to gain forgiveness.[6]

This revival was a step in the conversion process, that of inward reflection where the convert undergoes a process of conceiving the unseen to operate in or through the subject. The result can be the outburst of charismatic tendencies, visions, hallucinations, etc. The revival among Nigerian Adventists was considered a sign of the end-time where false spirits and "false christs" will deceive many to veer them off the course of the parousia. Thus, this type of movement was highly discouraged and quelled by Adventist leaders.

5. Lindenfeld, "Indigenous Encounters with Christian Missionaries."
6. Izima, *Brief History*, 23–24.

However, what foreign Adventists failed to understand was that in the Igbo worldview, the cosmos as we have it is populated by benevolent and malevolent spirits. Malevolent spirits can cause misfortune, wreak havoc, and hinder progress in individual and communal lives. Being able to control the cosmos and knowing the cause of misfortune is a prime preoccupation of their metaphysics. Hence, their recourse to magic and divination to gain power from the benevolent spirits to protect them from unseen evil forces. It should not be a surprise that the movement in 1938 was only a deeper yearning for the power of God through the Holy Spirit to permeate the practicality of the new Adventist faith.

The converts who experienced the charismatic renewal understood the Adventist theory of spiritual gifts in their own context by tapping into the power of the Holy Spirit. As a result, they were able to see visions (the unseen) and had power to heal and to overcome evil forces. Nonetheless, this vision was not shared by the mission leaders who possibly did not fully understand the Nigerian metaphysics and the lived realties of indigenous life. For them, this was not conversion but deceit. But for the Igbo Adventists, this was full adaptation or Africanization of Adventism from below, an original process which carted for the metaphysis of Igbo Adventists.

THE PRESENT STATE OF ADVENTISM IN NIGERIA[7]

If the Nigerian response to missionary Adventism saw lots of acceptance, some dichotomization, and then attempts towards Africanization, what happened to the denominational culture after the missionaries left? What did the Nigerian Adventists do in the face of socioreligious change? In this section it will be shown that Nigeria was rocked by a different sociopolitical framework that saw the rise of corruption such that the government became distrusted. In the wake of a highly galvanized corrupt system, the kind of church

---

7. The data and argument presented in this section stems from ethnographic research in Nigeria from 2016 to 2019.

that developed in response to the nation's abuses had to assure the populace of a better life, one that was infused with the very tones of the Nigerian neo-Pentecostal movement.

Nigerian Pentecostalism became a significant force in the religious landscape of Nigeria and beyond in the 1970s. It grew rapidly in recent decades and has had a profound impact on Nigerian society, culture, and politics. Pentecostalism emphasizes the personal experience of God's power and presence, and this has resonated with many Nigerians who sought hope, meaning, and purpose in their lives. Nigerian Pentecostalism has also been a catalyst for social change, empowering individuals and communities to challenge the status quo and work for justice and equality. Overall, Nigerian Pentecostalism is an important movement that is shaping the religious and cultural landscape of Nigeria and has the potential to impact the world. In Nigeria, one pervasive impact is that of the charismatization or Pentecostalization of mission-initiated churches or denominations, including Nigerian Adventism.

The Nigerian Adventist response to that kind Christianity came in three ways: adaptation of Pentecostal praxis, the full-blown Pentecostalization of Adventism, and the move to preserve Adventism.

Adaptation

The adaptation of Pentecostal praxis into Adventist worship began in the 1970s and 1980s in the wake of the campus revivals that rocked Nigeria. As a result, Nigeria experienced a significant growth in Pentecostal Christianity. Pentecostalism emphasized the power of the Holy Spirit and the need for personal spiritual experience, and it quickly gained popularity among Nigerians. The revivals saw the springing up of several charismatic student movements that metamorphosed into Pentecostal churches.[8] Nigerian Adventist students were not left out.

---

8. Ojo, "Pentecostalism and Charismatic Movements"; Ojo, "Deeper Life Christian Ministry"; Ojo, "Deeper Life Bible Church."

When they saw the lively worship atmosphere of the revivals in their campuses, they caught the born-again awakening. They were the second generation of Nigerian Adventists. They argued that their groups were overly formal in their worship. They wanted their worship to be authentic, lively, and relevant in the context they were in. This led to a historic revival among Adventist young people as charismatic practices in the wake of revivals among Adventist students became visible.

Soon, the effect was seen in many Nigerian congregations in the West of Nigeria. All-night prayers, vibrant worship styles, and music with percussion were adopted. Interestingly, at some point there was support for this movement by the Nigerian national leaders for a while until the student leaders who spearheaded this adaptation went for further studies abroad.

Pentecostalization

In a couple of years, those who were involved in adapting Pentecostal practices in Adventist churches, who went abroad for further studies, came back to Nigeria and took leadership positions. Especially at Babcock University (BU), Israel Olaore, a leading member of the aforementioned campus revival, became the university pastor. During his leadership, some Adventist leaders in BU started incorporating Pentecostal praxis in their worship spaces or student groups in reaction to complaints by majority non-Adventist students that Adventists were perceived as being too rigid and formal. This action could be interpreted as an effort to increase competition in a market for religions.

However, since most of the students were not actually Adventists, this move was not a consequence of losing members. As my interviews demonstrate, it was an effort to stay relevant (in terms of worship praxis) by including the same goods sold in the Nigerian religious market which was mainly Pentecostal. But this was another form of adaptation of Pentecostalism to Adventism. Soon a full-blown innovation, that of the Pentecostalization of Nigerian Adventism, was in place.

The Pentecostalization of Adventism was spearheaded also by other leaders who experienced the campus revival like Bukky Ajide. When he returned from the United States, he became a pastor in Lagos where he fostered the planting of a new congregation that has been branded a Pentecostal Adventist church. From then onwards, several other congregations have been planted in Lagos, Abuja, Port Harcourt, and Aba.

The Pentecostalization of Adventism developed because of the dissatisfaction with the traditional ways of worship found in the denomination's missionary-founded status quo. Moreover, the despair brought on by the collapse of the Nigerian state sparked the movement. Some Nigerian Adventists wanted to also speak against the political despair. In an effort to present a different social and religious order, they looked for creative methods to address the needs of society. Thus, some novel practices have helped Pentecostalize Adventism: the novelty of prayers, worship, liturgy, and prosperity preaching.

Prosperity preaching is an interesting pathway pursued by Pentecostal Adventists. They take elements of the Adventist tradition and fit them into an essentially neo-Pentecostal worldview. A major route used by this group is seeing the Sabbath as a key element to prosperity in the present and the future kingdom. By keeping the seventh-day Sabbath, these kinds of Adventist congregations claim that believers can unlock unknown secrets of prosperity even as they prepare themselves for the coming kingdom. This is known among them as "kingdom enterprise."[9] Arguably, this hermeneutic of linking the Sabbath to prosperity in the here and now and the hereafter is evidence of how a significant number of Nigerian Adventists are appropriating Adventist eschatology in a Pentecostal religious market. They do this by centering on the blessings of Sabbath observance, which is lacking in Nigerian Pentecostalism.

---

9. See booklet by Ajide, *Unknown Secrets of Prosperity*.

Preservation

The reaction of many Adventists to the adaptation of Pentecostal praxis in Adventist ethos, as well as Pentecostalization of Adventism, was a move towards preservation of missionary Adventism or Adventist heritage. The need for the preservation of Adventism's core beliefs was critical given that the Christian religious landscape in Nigeria was unidirectional or leaning towards Pentecostalism. The bulk of Adventists in Nigeria were worried about preserving the denomination's identity and any remaining missionary-transferred traditions. This is not shocking at all. Congregations naturally assume a functional status when confronted with change, in which they consider preserving their identity and organizational self-understanding. As a consequence, the church starts to view itself in functional terms and feels that it has a duty to serve God in the world.[10]

For these Adventists, the purpose of the church is to warn and prepare the world for the parousia—the end of the world. This implies a break from other churches that do not observe the Sabbath and do not conduct their worship services in a way that shows awe toward God. Therefore, mixing with other religions and permitting their practices among Adventists would be considered a rejection of the church's fundamental mission or of its functional identity. Because of this, most Nigerian Adventists embodied the idea that they were a remnant and thus branded the revival as false. Instead, the promotion of hymn-singing, orderly worship ethos, end-time apocalyptic teachings, and the distribution of media from American Adventists was resorted to.

A CRISIS OF IDENTITY?

The responses of Nigerians to Adventist missionaries and the later responses of Nigerian Adventists to Pentecostalization attest that Nigerian Adventism has become a local initiative of a global denomination. This initiative, that of a seemingly enculturated faith,

10. Van Gelder, "Rethinking Denominations."

appears to be in a state of identity crisis as the present state of Nigerian Adventism reveals. The identity crisis argument comes when one looks at what Adventism today is and asks: Where is Nigerian Adventism really going? Are they going back to missionary Adventism or are they concerned with relevancy in today's Nigeria? Other factors such as dichotomization or multiple religious belonging, church politics and policy application, tribalism, and nepotism have not made the case any better.

As Gabriel Masfa notes in his book on Adventism in Africa, some of the issues above threaten the identity of the larger African Adventist body. His lists relate well with Nigerian Adventism: polygamy; the church's responses to its youth's dealing with the postmodern world interpretation and application of Ellen White's writings; the interpretation of the Bible and its application to African culture; gender issues and their relation to Church missions; and Muslim-Adventist relations.[11] In view of this identity crisis, the question is: What can the future of Nigerian Adventism look like?

THE PROMISE OF NIGERIAN ADVENTISM

My way of responding to this follows thus. In his futuristic projections of Global South Christianity, Philip Jenkins in *The Next Christendom* argues that Christianity will become a religion of Africa. While this is already playing out for global Christianity, global Adventism is increasingly becoming an African denomination, especially in numbers. In this process, I suggest Nigerian Adventism has a role to play. Nigerian Adventism has had a unique history. From its early inception to facing the Civil War, political turmoil, military juntas, and Pentecostalization, Nigerian Adventism has seen a calamity of socioreligious change, adaptations, and innovations. Therefore, Nigerian Adventism can serve as beacon of an authentic faith that is in a crisis of staying with its denominational tradition or finding its own innovative pathways for the rest of African Adventism. In serving as a beacon, the elements of

---

11. Masfa, *Seventh-Day Adventism in Africa*, 167.

glocality and diversity must be highlighted. Moreover, authentic theological thinking and contextual missionizing cannot be overlooked in the overall discourse. I will now turn to these points.

Nigerian Adventism as Beacon for the Rest of Africa

The crisis of identity which was pointed out earlier is a good thing as its shows that Nigerian Adventism is in a constant flow of engagement between missionary traditions, Nigerian Christianity, and Nigerian culture. In this vein, Nigerian Adventism can serve as a model for other Adventist communities in the African region, demonstrating effective strategies for evangelism, discipleship, and community engagement in a very fast-paced world with constant social change. Nigerian Adventists can also help to promote unity and cooperation among Adventist communities in Africa by sharing resources and best practices, and by fostering a spirit of collaboration and partnership. Adventism in Nigeria has the potential to be a powerful force for positive change and growth within African Adventism.

The Glocal Nature of Nigerian Adventism

The term "glocal" is often used in discussions of globalization, and the impact of global forces on local. Glocality describes the way in which global ideas and trends are adapted and localized to fit a particular cultural, social, and economic context. At the same time, glocality also recognizes the ways in which local cultures and practices can influence and shape global trends.

Nigerian Adventism, though in an identity crisis, has been able to blend a world religion, that of Adventism, with local particularity. This has been shown through empirical study of ordinary Adventists in Nigeria's ecclesial practices. The end of missionary dominance and the development of new Adventist generations are significant elements causing the reinvention of worship rituals, even though the process of sorting through the inherited denominational culture is still ongoing. Yet, Adventism is experiencing many forms of appropriation at the grassroots level, just like Christianity in general. This process should not be truncated but studied and encouraged into the future so that the various "Adventisms" that will develop in the future will be as unique as Christianity itself which transcends ethnic, national, and cultural barriers.

The Diverse Nature of Nigerian Adventism

Close to the glocal nature of Nigerian Adventism is its diversity which encourages heterogeneity rather than global homogeneity. This can play out in various forms if the trend is encouraged. One way this can play out is for Nigerian Adventism to adapt and innovate General Conference calendars and programs rather than replicate ideas and programs without taking the cultural and local dynamics into consideration. At the same time, local initiatives and programs of Nigerian Adventism can be developed and suggested to other regions of Adventism for consideration if not adaptation. Thus, diversity becomes the right arm of glocality.

The Need for Authentic Theological Thinking in Nigerian Adventism

What then follows diversity of denominational praxis is theological thinking. Nigerian Adventists have many DMin-holders and several PhD-holders in the biblical studies, history, and theology. However, until now, religious materials from the United States and Europe are the main resource for theological thinking in Nigeria. With the contextual practices from below, Nigerian Adventist theologians and pastors need to start thinking as well from below and not from above. This includes dealing with the issues mentioned above that cause identity crisis as well as constructing liturgical theologies for the local context. One major area that needs constructive theological thinking is the Sabbath School.

While the official quarterly guide should not be thrown away, a theological commentary on the weekly lesson may assist local assimilation and help to deal with everyday issues of faith and praxis. Interestingly, on the Sabbath School, I must submit that Nigeria has gone backward instead of forward. In the past, there used to be contextual translations of the Sabbath School guide to various languages. Those translations are dwindling as English has become the preferred language of worship and God-talk.

Contextual Missionizing of Adventist Belief in Nigeria

Because Nigerian Adventism is actively undergoing a process where the gospel is being proclaimed and contextualized to every nation, tribe, language, and people (Rev 14:6), or in Adventist vocabulary, engaging the "Present Truth," contextual missionizing should be preferred. Rather than transplantation of preachers and teachers from the United States or abroad, preachers and mission practitioners should encourage translation (both in the linguistic and theological sense) and adaptation. Contextual missionizing needs to be faithful first to Scripture, and then to Adventist tradition and context. It is then that theology becomes truly contextual. When Nigerian Adventists encourage this, they will be able to develop a significant range of contextual approaches, not only in terms of actual thought, but also with regard to "method" and types or reasoning.

Young Church with Youthful Energy

Nigeria has one of the largest youth populations in the world. Correspondingly, Nigerian Adventism is predominantly a young church with youthful energy. Since Adventism has a strong focus on youth ministry, emphasis on engaging and empowering young people promises a vibrant kind of Adventism that can continue to grow and thrive. This possibility has been continuously truncated since the promise of young leaders being leaders of tomorrow has not been fully delivered.

The potential of allowing younger Nigerian Adventists in leadership positions and theological thinking will inject fresh ideas and perspectives that can help the church grow and develop in new and exciting ways. Furthermore, by harnessing the enthusiastic passion of the younger generation, the Adventist Church in Nigeria can reach out to more young people and bring them into the church. Since young people are often open to new ideas and willing to experiment with new approaches, Nigerian Adventism can harvest innovative and creative ways of doing mission and practicing church, which can help the church adapt to the changing needs and contexts of the society.

CONCLUSION

Adventism in Nigeria has a unique history and a dynamic development in its theology and practices. The responses of Nigerians to Adventism have been influenced by the approaches of Adventist Western missionaries and the distinctive history and development of the Nigerian socioreligious sphere. The adaptation of Pentecostal practices into Adventism has led to opposing responses of preservation and Pentecostalization, creating a seeming identity crisis. Yet, through the lens of *Nkeiruka*, the belief that the future holds brighter possibilities, this tension need not signal decay but rather a call toward transformation. As already argued, there is a need for developing a Nigerian Adventism that reflects the country's unique cultural and religious context. This Nigerian Adventism should be grounded in the original doctrines and practices of Adventism as it develops its authentic voice in Nigerian culture and thought patterns. A Nigerian Adventism rooted in its original doctrines yet consciously evolving within its cultural context can embody *Nkeiruka* as a theological and historiographical guide: moving forward with hope, contextual depth, and spiritual resilience to forge an authentic and vibrant Adventist identity in Nigeria.

Bibliography

2025 Annual Statistical Report of the General Conference of Seventh-day Adventists. New Series. Advance Release of Membership Statistics by Division for 2024. Silver Spring, MD: Office of Archives, Statistics, and Research, 2025.

Abar, Emmanuel M. "Islam, Christianity, Traditional Religions and Power Politics in Northern Nigeria Since Pre-Islamic Period." PhD diss., Andrews University, 2019.

Abodunde, Ayodeji. *A Heritage of Faith: A History of Christianity in Nigeria*. Lagos: Pierce Watershed, 2017.

Adeogun, Caleb, Jr. "Adeogun, Caleb Oyelayo (1932–2016)." Encyclopedia of Seventh-day Adventists, February 9, 2021. https://encyclopedia.adventist.org/article?id=FD4J.

Agboola, David T. "Golden Jubilee." *Advent Messenger* (1973) 4, 12.

———. *Seventh-day Adventist History in West Africa (1888–1988): A Mustard Seed*. Self-published, 2001.

———. *Seventh-day Adventists in Yorubaland, 1914–1964: A History of Christianity in Nigeria*. Ibadan: Daystar, 1987.

Ajayi, J. F. Ade. *Christian Missions in Nigeria, 1841–1891: The Making of a New Elite*. London: Longman, 1965.

Ajide, Bukola. *The Unknown Secrets of Prosperity*. Lekki: Victory Sanctuary Seventh-day Adventist Church, n.d.

Alalade, Adekunle A. *Limiting Factors to the Success of the Seventh-day Adventist Church in Africa*. Ibadan: Agbo Areg, 2008.

Alao, Dayo, ed. *90 Years of Adventism in Nigeria, 1914–2004: A Compendium*. Lagos: Communication Department of Seventh-day Adventist Church in Nigeria, 2004.

Anonaba, Kingsley Chukwuemeka. "Onyeodo. Daniel Ogbonna (1885–1969)." Encyclopedia of Seventh-day Adventists, September 18, 2024. https://encyclopedia.adventist.org/article?id=DJOW.

Andross, Matilda Erickson. *Story of the Advent Message*. Washington, DC: Review and Herald, 1926.

Anosike, Luke U. "The Development of the Seventh-day Adventist Church in Southeast Nigeria." Term paper, Andrews University, 1971.

Arewa House Archives. (A.H.A.), Kaduna, 15246.

Ayandele, E. A. *The Missionary Impact on Modern Nigeria, 1842–1914: A Political and Social Analysis*. London: Longman, 1966.

Babalola, David O. *Sweet Memories of Our Pioneers*. Lagos: Emahine Repro Graphics, 2001.

Babalola, James A. O. "An Assessment of the Impact of Charismatic Movement on the Unity of the Seventh-day Adventist Church in South-Western Nigeria (1982–2016)." PhD diss., Olabisi Onabanjo University, 2018.

Babatunde, S. O. "Adventists at the University of Ibadan." *West African Advent Messenger* (1970) 1.

Babcock, David C. "Trials and Victories." *Advent Review and Sabbath Herald* (1919) 24.

———. "The Work in West Africa." *Advent Review and Sabbath Herald* (1909) 15–16.

Barnes, Andrew E. "'Evangelization Where It Is Not Wanted': Colonial Administrators and Missionaries in Northern Nigeria During the First Third of the Twentieth Century." *Journal of Religion in Africa* 25 (1995) 412–41.

Bartlett, W. T. "A United Missions Council." *Advent Survey* (1939) 1–2.

Bassey, Magnus O. "Missionary Rivalry and Educational Expansion in Southern Nigeria, 1885–1932." *The Journal of Negro Education* 60 (1991) 36–46. https://doi.org/10.2307/2295531.

Bauman, Herman. *African Safari for Jesus*. N.p.: Xlibris, 2008.

Baur, John. *2000 Years of Christianity in Africa: An African Church History*. Nairobi: Paulines, 1994.

Bediako, Kwame. *Christianity in Africa: The Renewal of a Non-Western Religion*. Maryknoll, NY: Orbis, 1995.

"Bible Sabbath Association Organizational Profile: Interview with The Joint Church of God 7th-Day Fellowship." *The Sabbath Sentinel*, September–October 1999, 12. https://www.biblesabbath.org/tss/479/tss_479.pdf.

Bosch, David J. *Transforming Mission: Paradigm Shifts in Theology of Mission*. Maryknoll, NY: Orbis, 1991.

Burgess, Richard. *Nigeria's Christian Revolution: The Civil War Revival and Its Pentecostal Progeny (1967–2006)*. Oxford: Regnum, 2008.

Campbell, Malcolm N. "West African Problems." *Missionary Worker*, July 6, 1921, 1.

Chow, Christie Chui-Shan. *Schism: Seventh-day Adventism in Post-Denominational China*. Notre Dame, IN: University of Notre Dame Press, 2021.

Christian, L. H. "The Annual Division Meeting." *Advent Survey* 3 (1931) 1–2.

Chucks, J. O. "New Branch Sabbath School." *West African Advent Messenger*, February/March 1971, 6.

Clarke, C. N. A., and C. N. M. Monsell. "Extract from P.C.J.140/1913—"Spheres of Influence of Missionary Societies." February 9, 1931; N. A. K. Jos Prof 120/1931.

Clifford, Jesse. "Camp-Meetings in Southern Nigeria." *Advent Survey*, May 1930, 3.

———. "Into South Nigeria, West Africa." *Advent Review and Sabbath Herald*, October 18, 1923, 13.

———. "Like a Grain of Mustard Seed." *Advent Review and Sabbath Herald*, May 29, 1930, 13–14.

———. "The Message in the Niger Delta." *Missions Quarterly*, 1930, 17–20.

———. "Southeast Nigeria." *Advent Review and Sabbath Herald*, August 11, 1927, 9.

———. "Troublous Times in West Africa." *Missionary Worker*, January 24, 1930, 8.

Coleman, James. *Nigeria: Background to Nationalism*. Berkeley: University of California Press, 1971.

Cookey, Scholastica Ahiazunwa, and Patricia Ngozi Ijioma. "A Panoramic Study of Names in Igbo Society." In *Politics and Identity Formation in Southeastern Nigeria: The Igbo in Perspective*, edited by Apollos O. Nwauwa and Ogechi E. Anyanwu, 17–30. Lanham, MD: Lexington, 2019.

Coon, Roger W. "General Conference Radio Secretary Tours Nigeria and Ghana." *West African Advent Messenger*, January 1958, 1.

Cormack, A. W. "Polygamy and Marriage Relationship." *Eastern Tidings*, September 1, 1926, 1.

Crampton, E. P. T. *Christianity in Northern Nigeria*. Zaria: Gaskiya, 1976.

Damsteegt, P. Gerard. *Foundations of the Seventh-day Adventist Message and Mission*. Grand Rapids: Eerdmans, 1977.

———. "Foundations of the Seventh-Day Adventist Message and Mission." *Missiology: An International Review* 8 (1980) 3–18.

Danmole, H. O. "Religion and Politics in Colonial Northern Nigeria: The Case of Ilorin Emirate." *Journal of Religious History* 16 (1990) 140–53.

Diara, Benjamin C., and George C. Nche. "European and American Christian Missions and Nigeria's National Development (1840–1960)." *Journal of Educational and Social Research* 3 (2013) 89–99.

Dick, E. D. "The West Coast of Africa." *Adventist Review*, August 17, 1993, 10.

Dioka, J. "Marriage in Igboland." BD thesis, Bigard Memorial Seminary, 1980.

Dodds, William. *Ibo Opening: The Story of a Primitive Methodist Missionary in Nigeria*. London: Epworth, 1952.

Editorial staff. "Our Relationship to Other Societies." *Advent Review and Sabbath Herald*, August 19, 1920, 5–6.

Egharevba, Jacob. *A History of Benin*. Ibadan: Ibadan University Press, 1968.

Ekechi, Felix K. *Missionary Enterprise and Rivalry in Igboland, 1857–1914*. London: Frank Cass, 1972.

Eregare, Emmanuel Orihentare. *An African Christian Church History: Seventh-day Adventist Cosmology in Edo/Delta States, 1948–2012, and Ecumenical Initiatives*. Lagos: Christ Coming, 2013.

———. *Groundwork of the Seventh-day Adventist Church History in Nigeria (1914–2014)*. Lagos: Freedom Network, 2024.

Eva, Duncan W. "Ahoada Hospital in Nigeria Nationalized on June 1." *Advent Review and Sabbath Herald*, June 22, 1972, 24.

Ezeigbo, Theodora Akachi. "Traditional Women's Institutions in Igbo Society: Implications for the Igbo Female Writer." *African Languages and Cultures* 3 (1990) 149–65.

Ezenwafor-Afuecheta, Chikelu I., and Ifeka J. Onyeocha. "The Dynamics of Name-Taking in Igbo Society." *OCHENDO: An African Journal of Innovative Studies* 2 (2021) 316–26.

Fall Council Action, 1930, 74–75, Box 3811, subject: Polygamy, General Conference Archives, Maryland, USA.

Falola, Toyin. *Violence in Nigeria: The Crisis of Religious Politics and Secular Ideologies*. Rochester: University of Rochester Press, 1998.

Falola, Toyin, and Bukola A. Oyeniyi. *Nigeria*. N.p.: ABC-CLIO, 2015.

Falola, Toyin, and Matthew M. Heaton. *A History of Nigeria*. Cambridge: Cambridge University Press, 2008.

Faught, C. Brad. "Missionaries, Indirect Rule, and the Changing Mandate of Mission in Colonial Northern Nigeria: The Case of Canada's Rowland Victor Bingham and the Sudan Interior Mission." *Journal of the Canadian Church Historical Society* 43 (2001) 147–69.

Fiedler, Klaus. "Christian Missions and Western Colonialism: Soulmates or Antagonists?" In *Faith at the Frontiers of Knowledge*, edited by Kenneth R. Ross, 239–58. Luviri Reprints 2. Malawi: Luviri, 2018.

Fly, James L. "African-Indian Ocean." *Adventist Review*, April 18, 1985, 27.

———. "ASWA: A Vision Still Aflame After 25 Years." *Adventist Review*, February 7, 1985, 20.

Foreign Mission Board. "Records of the Foreign Mission Board." January 21, 1903. General Conference of Seventh day Adventists Archives. https://documents.adventistarchives.org/Minutes/FMBM/FMBM19010424.pdf.

———. "Records of the Foreign Mission Board." May 2, 1902. General Conference of Seventh day Adventists Archives. https://documents.adventistarchives.org/Minutes/FMBM/FMBM19010424.pdf.

Galadima, Bulus Y., and Yusufu Turaki. "Christianity in Nigeria: Part I." *African Journal of Evangelical Theology* 20 (2001) 85–101.

General Conference Committee. "Minutes." April 1, 1910. http://documents.adventistarchives.org/Minutes/GCC/GCC1910.pdf.

———. "Minutes." April 1923. http://documents.adventistarchives.org/Minutes/GCC/GCC1923.pdf.

General Conference Department of Education, Seventh-day Adventist Church. *The Story of Our Church*. Washington, DC: Pacific, 1956.

General Conference of Seventh-day Adventists, ed. *Seventh-day Adventists Believe: A Biblical Exposition of Fundamental Doctrines*. Silver Spring, MD: Review and Herald, 2005.

George, Sam, and Godfrey Harold. "Motus Dei (The Move of God): A Theology and Missiology for a Moving World." *Pharos Journal of Theology* 102 (2021) 1–12. https://doi.org/10.46222/10216.

Gramlich, John. "Fast Facts About Nigeria and Its Immigrants as U.S. Travel Ban Expands." Pew Research Center, February 3, 2020. https://www.pewresearch.org/short-reads/2020/02/03/fast-facts-about-nigeria-and-its-immigrants-as-u-s-travel-ban-expands/.

Greenleaf, Floyd. *A Land of Hope: The Growth of the Seventh-day Adventist Church in South America*. Tatuí: Casa Publicadora Brasileira, 2011.

———. *The Seventh-day Adventist Church in Latin America and the Caribbean*. 2 vols. Berrien Springs, MI: Andrews University Press, 1992.

Hackett, Rosalind I. J. *Religion in Calabar: The Religious Life and History of a Nigerian Town*. Berlin: De Gruyter, 2013.

Hale, Dudley. "Gold Coast, West Africa." *Adventist Review*, December 20, 1906, 16.

Hartlapp, Johannes. *Siebenten-Tags-Adventisten im Nationalsozialismus: Unter Berücksichtigung der geschichtlichen und theologischen Entwicklung in Deutschland von 1875 bis 1950*. Göttingen: V&R Unipress, 2008.

Hastings, Adrian. *The Church in Africa, 1450–1950*. Oxford: Clarendon, 1994.

Heinz, Daniel. *Church, State, and Religious Dissent: A History of Seventh-day Adventists in Austria, 1890–1975*. Frankfurt am Main: Peter Lang, 1993.

———. *Ludwig Richard Conradi. Missionar der Siebenten-Tags-Adventisten in Europa*. Frankfurt am Main: Peter Lang, 1986.

Höschele, Stefan. *Christian Remnant—African Folk Church: Seventh-Day Adventism in Tanzania, 1903–1980*. Studies in Christian Mission 34. Leiden: Brill, 2007.

———. *From the End of the World to the Ends of the Earth: The Development of Seventh-day Adventist Missiology*. Vol. 6 of *Kachere Study*. Blantyre: CLAIM, 2004.

———. "Interchurch Relations in Seventh-Day Adventist History: A Study in Ecumenics." Habilitation, Charles University, 2016.

———. "To Baptize or Not to Baptize? Adventists and Polygamous Converts." *Africa Journal of Evangelical Theology* 34 (2015) 35–50.

Höschele, Stefan, and Chigemezi N. Wogu, eds. *Contours of European Adventism: Issues in the History of the Denomination on the Old Continent*. Adventistica, 2nd ser. Möckern-Friedensau: Institute of Adventist Studies, Friedensau Adventist University, 2020.

Hyatt, James M. "West Africa." *Advent Review and Sabbath Herald*, August 11, 1903, 19.

———. "West Africa." *Advent Review and Sabbath Herald*, August 31, 1905, 13.

Hyde, John J. N. A. K. Zar. Prof. C. 402 vol. 2; J. J. Hyde, Seventh-Day Adventist Mission Nigerian Branch, P.O. Box 19, Ibadan, a letter addressed to:

District Officer i/c Emirate Division, Zaria, April 20, 1931, N. A. K. Zar. Prof. C. 402 vol. 2.

———. "Progress in Northern Nigeria." *Advent Survey*, November 1936, 4.

Hyde, L. M. Fieldwork. Watford, 1994.

Igwe, Chidi. "Nkeiruka: The Challenges and Prospects of a Nation in Search of Recovery." Igbo Studies Association (blog), June 4, 2014. https://www.igbostudies.org/blogs/nkeiruka-the-challenges-and-prospects-of-a-nation-in-search-of-recovery.

Ilogu, Edmund. "Christianity and Ibo Traditional Religion." *International Review of Mission* 54 (1965) 335–42.

Isichei, Elizabeth. *A History of Christianity in Africa: From Antiquity to the Present*. London: SPCK, 1995.

Ising, Walter K. "Visiting West Africa." *Quarterly Review of the European Division of Seventh-day Adventists*, 1928, 4.

Iwuchukwu, Marinus C. *Muslim-Christian Dialogue in Post-Colonial Northern Nigeria: The Challenges of Inclusive Cultural and Religious Pluralism*. New York: Palgrave Macmillan, 2013.

Izima, David A. *A Brief History of the SDA Church in Eastern States of Nigeria*. Aba: Span, 1973.

Kalu, Ogbu U. *Christianity in West Africa: The Nigerian Story*. Ibadan: Daystar, 1978.

———. "The Shape and Flow of African Church Historiography." In *African Christianity: An African Story*, edited by Ogbu U. Kalu, 1–23. Trenton, NJ: Africa World Press, 2007.

Kaplan, Steven. "The Africanization of Missionary Christianity: History and Typology." In *Indigenous Responses to Western Christianity*, edited by Steven Kaplan, 9–27. New York: New York University Press, 1995.

Kern, M. E. "The Study of Our African Mission." *The Youth Instructor*, June 22, 1915, 14.

Knight, George R. "Adventist Theology 1844 to 1994." *Ministry*, August 1994, 5–7.

———. *The Fat Lady and the Kingdom*. Nampa, ID: Pacific, 1995.

Kolade, J. O. Y. "The Light Shines at the University of Ife." *West African Advent Messenger*, February/March 1971, 10.

Krum, Ronald E. "Directed by God's Providence." *Youth's Instructor*, April 2 and 9, 1968, 4–13.

Kuranga, Abraham A. "Seventh-day Adventism in Western Nigeria, 1914–81: A Study in the Relationship Between Christianity and African Culture from the Missionary Era to the Introduction of African Leadership." PhD diss., Miami University, 1992.

Langer, Richard C. "Kingdom Integration: Reflections on Premillennialism and Cultural Engagement." *Criswell Theological Review* 10 (2012) 29–30.

Lashier, S. J. "From West Africa." *North Pacific Union Gleaner*, July 17, 1924, 3.

Lawson, Ronald. "Sources of the Current Crisis in the World Church." *Spectrum*, December 14, 2018. https://spectrummagazine.org/views/sources-current-crisis-world-church.

Letter to the West African Union of SDA Church at Accra through Pastor G.M. Elmstrom: "An Inevitable Appeal at this Momentous Time of Our Religious Emancipation to All Our Delegates to Accra Conference of Seventh-day Adventist."

Langford, L. F. to E. E. Andross, August 23, 1920, Correspondences, Box 9864, General Conference of Seventhday Adventists Archives, Silver Spring, MD.

Linnel, Irving N. Letter to J. L. Shaw, June 9, 1921, Correspondences, Box 9864, General Conference of Seventhday Adventists Archives, Silver Spring, MD.

Lindenfeld, David. "Indigenous Encounters with Christian Missionaries in China and West Africa, 1800–1920: A Comparative Study." *Journal of World History* 16 (2005) 336.

Lugard, Frederick D. *The Dual Mandate in British Tropical Africa*. London: Frank Cass, 1965.

Maigadi, Ibrahim B. *The Adventist Church in Northern Nigeria: A Historical Source Material of Seventh-day Adventist Church in Nigeria*. Zaria: Culture Impressive, 2005.

Masfa, Gabriel. *Seventh-Day Adventism in Africa: A Historical Survey of the Interaction Between Religion, Traditions, and Culture*. 1st ed. London: Routledge, 2023.

———. *Seventh-Day Adventist Historiography: An Introduction*. Berlin: Peter Lang, 2021.

Maxwell, A. S. "Widening Horizons." *British Advent Messenger*, January 24, 1936, 1–2.

McClements, William. "Itinerating in Nigeria." *Advent Review and Sabbath Herald*, February 14, 1924, 12.

———. "Missionary Problems in Nigeria." *Present Truth and Signs of the Times*, October 8, 1925, 4.

———. "Nigeria." *Mission Quarterly*, 1932, 12.

———. "Nigerian Union Mission." *Advent Survey*, November 1930, 2.

———. "Our First Camp-Meeting in Nigeria." *Advent Survey*, August 1929, 6.

———. "The Outlook in Nigeria." *Advent Survey*, December 1936, 1.

———. "Pentecostal Experiences in Nigeria." *British Advent Messenger*, January 8, 1937, 7.

———. "Progress in the Nigerian Mission Field." *Advent Review and Sabbath Herald*, August 20, 1931, 9.

Mitchison, Lois. *Nigeria: Newest Nation*. London: Pall Mall, 1960.

Monsell, C. N. Acting Resident Plateau Province, "Seventh Day Adventist Mission—Establishment of."

National Archives of Kaduna. (N. A. K.) SNP 7, 3754/1911, (1930, 1931, 1932), Files and letters related to Christian Missions/Establishment of Seventh-day Adventist Mission. N. A. K. Jos Prof 120/1931.

N. A. K. Zar. Prof. 41, 1932.

N. A. K. Zar. Prof. C. 402 vol. 2.

N. A. K., "Minutes" in the Memorandum No 14432/11, from Secretary Northern Provinces, Kaduna, To Resident, Zaria Province, "1 March 1931, on Seventh-Day Adventist Mission—Establishment of."

Nengel, John G., and Chigemezi N. Wogu. "Colonial Politics, Missionary Rivalry, and the Beginnings of Seventh-Day Adventist Mission in Northern Nigeria." *Mission Studies* 38 (2021) 213–35.

Newmann, Las G. "The Caribbean's Response to the Great Commission: History and Models of Response." *Caribbean Journal of Evangelical Theology* 1 (1997) 21.

"News from All Over." *Australasian Record and Advent World Survey*, November 11, 1968, 5.

Nuefeld, Don, ed. "Nigeria Mission." In *Seventh-day Adventist Encyclopedia*, 181. 2nd ed. Hagerstown: Review and Herald, 1996.

———. *Seventh-day Adventist Encyclopedia*. 2 vols. 2nd ed. Hagerstown: Review and Herald, 1996.

Njoku, Moses. "A History of Seventh-day Adventist Church in Igboland (1923–2010)." PhD diss., University of Nigeria Nsukka, 2014.

Nnoroviele, Salome C. *The Way People Live—Life Among the Ibo Women of Nigeria*. San Diego: Lucent, 1998.

Nwadialor, Kanayo. "Christian Missionary Enterprise and the Background to Nationalism in Nigeria, 1870–1960." *Igwebuike: An African Journal of Arts and Humanities* 1 (2015) 11–20.

Nyekwere, David. *Medical Institutions of the Seventh-day Adventist in Southeastern Nigeria: An Instrument of Evangelism 1940-2000*. Lagos: Natural Prints, 2004.

Ojo, Matthews A. "The Charismatic Movement in Nigeria Today." *International Bulletin of Missionary Research* 19 (1995) 114–18.

———. "Deeper Life Bible Church in Nigeria." In *New Dimension in African Christianity*, edited by Paul Gifford, 135–56. Nairobi: All African Council of Churches, 1992.

———. "Deeper Life Christian Ministry: A Case Study of the Charismatic Movement in Western Nigeria." *Journal of Religion in Africa* 18 (1988) 141–68.

———. *The End-Time Army: Charismatic Movements in Modern Nigeria*. Trenton, NJ: Africa, 2006.

———. "Pentecostalism and Charismatic Movements in Nigeria: Factors of Growth and Inherent Challenges." *Renewal* 3 (2016) 74–94.

Oliver, Barry David. *Principles for Reorganization of the Seventh-day Adventist Administrative Structure, 1888–1903: Implications for an International Church*. PhD diss., Andrews University, 1989.

Onwuzurigbo, Okorobia. "Igbo Marriage and Family Life." *Sacra Theologia* 18 (1990) 469–72.

Oosterwal, Gottfried. *Mission: Possible*. Silver Spring, MD: Review and Herald, 1972.

BIBLIOGRAPHY

O'Reggio, Trevor. "The Early Adventist Mission to Jamaica." *Journal of the Adventist Theological Society* 28 (2017) 81–98.

Owusu-Mensa, Kofi. "Clifford, Jesse." Dictionary of African Christian Biography, 2001. https://dacb.org/stories/ghana/clifford-jesse/.

———. *Saturday God and Adventism in Ghana*. New York: Peter Lang, 1993.

Paulien, Jon. "The Best Is Yet to Come: A Vision for the Eschatological Remnant." The Battle of Armageddon, August 2024. https://www.thebattleofarmageddon.com/wp-content/uploads/2024/08/The-Open-Remnant.pdf.

Pew Research Center's Forum on Religion & and Public Life Global Christianity. "Global Christianity: A Report on the Size and Distribution of the World's Christian Population." Pew-Templeton Global Religious Futures Project. December 2011. http://www.pewforum.org/files/2011/12/Christianity-fullreport-web.pdf.

———. "Nigeria." Pew-Templeton Global Religious Futures Project. http://www.globalreligiousfutures.org/countries/nigeria/religiousdemography#/?affiliations_religion_1d=0&affiliations_year=2010.

Playfair 1931: N. A. K. Zar. Prof. 41, 1932.

"Polygamy." General Conference Session Action, 1926, Box 3811, subject: Polygamy, General Conference Archives, Silver Spring MD.

Post, Kenneth, and Michael Vickers. *Structure and Conflict in Nigeria 1960–1966*. Madison, WI: University of Wisconsin Press, 1973.

Read, W. E. "Itinerating in Nigeria." *Advent Survey*, June 1930, 3.

———. "Itinerating in Southern Nigeria." *Advent Review and Sabbath Herald*, May 5, 1927, 18–19.

———. "The Message in Nigeria." *Advent Review and Sabbath Herald*, August 7, 1930, 14.

Reynaud, Daniel. "Understanding History: Seventh-day Adventists and Their Perspectives." *TEACH Journal of Christian Education* 10 (2016) 54–62.

Sabbath School Lesson Quarterly. First Quarter, 1938, 11–17. https://documents.ad ventistarchives.org/SSQ/SS19380101-01.pdf.

Samson, Jane. "The Problem of Colonialism in the Western Historiography of Christian Missions." *Religious Studies and Theology* 23 (2004) 3–25.

Sanneh, Lamin. *West African Christianity*. Maryknoll, NY: Orbis, 1983.

Serns, Arthur. E. Letter to J. L. Shaw, October 3, 1920. Correspondences, Box 9864, General Conference of Seventhday Adventists Archives, Silver Spring, MD.

Seventh day Adventist Yearbook. Washington, DC: Review and Herald, 1906.

Seventh day Adventist Yearbook. Washington, DC: Review and Herald, 1907.

Seventh day Adventist Yearbook. Washington, DC: Review and Herald, 1914.

Seventh day Adventist Yearbook. Washington, DC: Review and Herald, 1932.

Shankar, Shobana. *Who Shall Enter Paradise? Christian Origins in Muslim Northern Nigeria, Ca. 1890–1975*. Athens, OH: Ohio University Press, 2014.

Shinmyo, Tadaomi. "A History in Missiological Perspective of the Seventh-day Adventist Church in Japan from 1945 to 1985." DMin diss., Andrews University, 1987.
Thompstone, E. W. Secretary Northern Provinces, to Resident, Zaria Province, on Seventh Day Adventist Mission, August 27, 1931.
Tikili, Benjamin I. "Experiences and Convictions." *Columbian Union Visitor*, June 2, 1938, 1–2.
Till, W. G. "Advance on the Nigerian Front." *Advent Review and Sabbath Herald*, December 4, 1930, 21.
Trim, David J. B. *Hearts of Faith: How We Became Seventh-day Adventists*. Nampa, ID: Pacific, 2022.
———. *A Passion for Mission*. Bracknell, UK: Newbold Academic, 2019.
Trim, David J. B., and Daniel Heinz, eds. *Parochialism, Pluralism, and Contextualization: Challenges to Adventist Mission in Europe (19th–21st Centuries)*. Frankfurt am Main: Peter Lang, 2010.
Turner, W. G. "Put Biafra in Your Prayers." *Australasian Record and Advent World Survey*, October 7, 1968, 8.
Ubah, C. N. "Christian Missionary Penetration of the Nigerian Emirates, with Special Reference to the Medical Missions Approach." *Muslim World* 57 (1987) 17–18.
Ukegbu, J. O. "The Blessedness of Communion with God." *Advent Messenger*, April/May 1973, 12.
Van Allen, Judith. "Aba Riots or the Igbo Women's War? Ideology, Stratification and the Invisibility of Women." *Ufahamu: A Journal of African Studies* 6 (1975) 11–41.
Van Gelder, Craig. "Rethinking Denominations and Denominationalism in Light of a Missional Ecclesiology." *Word & World* 25 (2005) 23–33.
Vine, Mary J. "A New Song." *Present Truth*, January 5, 1933, 11–12.
———. "Marriage in the Ibo Country: A Great Mission Problem." *Present Truth*, January 5, 1933, 15.
Walls, Andrew F. *The Cross-Cultural Process in Christian History*. Maryknoll, NY: Orbis, 2002.
Walls, Andrew F., and Christopher Fyfe. *Christianity in Africa in the 1990s*. Edinburgh: Centre for African Studies, University of Edinburgh, 1996.
Wariboko, Nimi. *Nigerian Pentecostalism*. Rochester, NY: University of Rochester Press, 2014.
Watson, Noelle. "Benin City Nigeria." In *International Dictionary of Historical Places: Middle East and Africa*, edited by Trudy Ring et al., 4:125. Chicago, IL: Fitzroy Dearborn, 1996.
White, Ellen G. *Life Sketches of Ellen G. White*. Mountain View, CA: Pacific, 1915.
William, Timothy Jones. "The Missionaries' Position: Polygamy and Divorce in the Anglican Communion, 1888–1988." *Journal of Religious History* 35 (2011) 393–408.
Williams, DeWitt S. *Precious Memories of Missionaries of Color* 2. Nampa, ID: TEACH Services, 2015.

BIBLIOGRAPHY

Wilson, Neal C. "What Is It Like—To Starve?" *North Pacific Union Gleaner*, November 18, 1968, 1.

Wogu, Chigemezi N. "The Development of Adventist Missiology." In *The Oxford Handbook of Seventh-day Adventism*, edited by Michael W. Campbell et al., 371–85. Oxford: Oxford University Press, 2024. https://doi.org/10.1093/oxfordhb/9780197502297.013.24.

———. "Independence, Civil War, and the Beginnings of Indigenization of Seventh-day Adventism in Nigeria from the 1940s to 1990s." *Spes Christiana* 34 (2023) 91–116.

———. *A Passion for Mission*. Bracknell, UK: Newbold Academic, 2019.

———. "Preparing Converts for the Second Coming of Christ: The Encounter of Seventh-day Adventist Missionaries with Indigenous Issues in Nigeria from 1900 to the 1940s." *Spes Christiana* 31 (2020) 85–108.

———. "Trailblazers of Adventism in Nigeria, 1900s–1930s." *Journal of Adventist Mission Studies* 15 (2019) 1–13.

Wosu, Robert O. "Our Relation to Political Organizations." *West African Advent Messenger*, November 1951, 3.

Index

90 Years, 35–36, 82, 96

Aba, 34, 38–39, 45, 73, 78–80, 87, 90, 105, 125, 129, 142
Aba Government School, 33
Abar, Emmanuel M., 52, 137
Abaribe, Robert, 38–39
Aba Riots, 75, 79, 146
Abeokuta, 108
Abodunde, 95, 137
Abua, 81
Abuja, 129
Accra, 101, 143
Accra Conference, 143
acculturation, 77
actions, 51, 61, 82–84, 86, 103, 128
   defer, 62
   definite, 63
   divine, 24
activities
   evangelistic, 7, 38
   political, 80
   revivalist, 114
   social, 80
   student movement, 96
ACWA, 108
Adaelu, 38
Adamawa Province, 56
adaptability, 16

adaptation, x, 10, 13, 120, 126–28, 131, 133–35
   local, 4, 13–14
Adeboye, Enoch, 115
Adekunle A., 137
Adeogun, 101, 113–14
   Caleb Oyelayo, 113, 137
Adeogun Jr., 113
administration, 51–52, 56, 114
   colonial, 49, 56
administrative structures, 13
administrators, 55–56, 105
Adventism, 2–5, 21–23, 25, 29, 33, 38–39, 41–47, 71–75, 88, 92–93, 95–96, 114–25, 127–35
   arrival of, 72, 107
   dichotomized, 124
   global, 16, 131
   growth of, 40, 94
   indigenization of, 95–96
   international, x
   left, 39, 87
   local, 16
   localizing, 40, 90
   mission historiography of, 14, 25
   mission history of, 43, 96
   opposition, 46
   professed, 88

149

Adventism (continued)
  progress of, 118
  rooting, 26, 30
  ushered, 9
Adventism in Africa, ix, 14–16,
  131, 143
Adventism in Nigeria, 2, 25, 29–30,
  42, 45, 74, 94–96, 118–20,
  126, 132, 135, 137
Adventism's missiological
  quadrilateral, 74
Adventist beliefs, 4, 33, 73, 134
Adventist Biafran soldiers, 106
Adventist body, 82, 124
Adventist Church in Northern
  Nigeria, 27, 29, 41, 67, 143
Adventist circles, 87, 108–9
Adventist clinic, 121
Adventist College of West Africa,
  97, 108
Adventist communities, 132
Adventist congregations, 82, 84
Adventist congregations claim, 129
Adventist conviction, 70
Adventist core epistemology, 3
Adventist counterparts, 115
Adventist denomination, 99, 106, 109
Adventist doctrines, 8, 10
Adventist ecclesial praxis, 118
Adventist education, 78
Adventist ethos, 92, 130
Adventist faith, 4, 34, 83, 89, 110,
  122, 126
Adventist heritage, 130
Adventist High School, 97
Adventist historians, 8, 11, 73, 102
Adventist historiography, x–xi, 9,
  12, 23
Adventist history, x, 9, 25–27
Adventist homes, 76
Adventist identity, 9, 121
  vibrant, 135
Adventist leaders, 57, 90–91, 125, 128

Adventist message, x, 33, 36, 83,
  85–88, 122
Adventist ministers, 67, 73
Adventist missiology, 8, 147
Adventist mission, ix, xi, 9–11, 14,
  26–27, 33, 36, 43–45, 47,
  63–64, 67–68, 73–74, 80, 122
  juxtaposing, 10
  volume frames, 21
Adventist mission agenda, 10
Adventist missionaries, x–xi, 27,
  44, 46–47, 68–70, 73–77,
  80–82, 91–93, 95–96, 100,
  124–25
  female, 71
  first, 30–31
  unknown key pioneer, 29
Adventist missionaries in Nigeria,
  29, 47, 86, 92–93
Adventist missionary activities, 96
Adventist missionary catechesis, 118
Adventist missionary engagements,
  70
Adventist mission enterprise, 42, 71
Adventist mission growth, xi
Adventist mission historiography,
  7, 10–12, 15–17, 27, 92–93
Adventist mission historiography in
  Europe, 12, 14
Adventist mission historiography in
  Nigeria, 3, 21, 26
Adventist mission history, 5, 9–10,
  13, 15–17, 43, 92–93
Adventist mission history in
  Nigeria, 1–2, 96
Adventist mission in Nigeria, 27,
  57, 76, 92
Adventist mission in northern
  Nigeria, 45–67
Adventist press, 121
Adventist Review, 139–41
Adventist revivals, 111
Adventist rituals, 84

INDEX

Adventists, 7–8, 12, 22–24, 33–35, 38–39, 45–46, 48–49, 57–59, 61, 63–66, 68–70, 72–74, 81–88, 90–91, 104–11, 113–14, 116–19, 121–25, 128, 130
  ardent, 34
  cultural, 110
  foreign, 126
  formal, 37
  lone, 34
  ordinary, 89, 132
  preceded, 121
  reevaluating, 9
  second-generation, 109
  vibrant, 110
  young, 109–10
Adventist Sabbath School lesson, 87
Adventist scholarship, 11
Adventist school, 39, 123
Adventists in Nigeria, ix, 96, 108, 117, 130
Adventist sociologist, 116
Adventist story, 47
Adventist Student Fellowships (ASF), 108
Adventist studies, 141
Adventist system, 81
Adventist theology, ix, 10, 142
Adventist theory of spiritual gifts, 89, 126
Adventist top-tier body, 84
Adventist traditions, 119, 129, 134
Adventist Welfare Service, 105
Adventist workers, 42, 44, 81, 90
  indigenous, 98
  local, 94, 117
Adventist world/ideology, 121
Adventist worship, 127
Adventist Youth Ministries, 116
Advent Messenger, 137, 146
Advent Printing Press, 74
Advent Review and Sabbath Herald, 32, 138–41, 143, 145–46
Advent Survey, 90, 138–39, 142–43, 145
Advent Survey3, 138
Africa, 3, 12, 14–18, 37, 48, 70, 75, 95–96, 102, 119, 131–32, 137, 144
  sub-Saharan, 95, 102
Africa interior, 48
African Adventism, 131–32
African Adventist body, 131
African agency, 19
African Christian, x, 18–20, 145
African Christianity, 17–19, 26, 142
African Church Historiography, 17, 142
  modern, 18
  situating, 18
African cultures, 70, 131, 142
African denomination, 131
African Folk Church, 70, 141
African historian Ogbu Kalu, x
African identity, 125
African Independent Churches, 20
African-Indian Ocean, 113, 140
African indigenous cultures, 77
Africanization, 16, 78, 84, 122, 125–26
Africanization of Adventism, 125–26
Africanization of Missionary Christianity, 70, 142
African Mission, 36, 142
African missionaries, x, 36
  indigenous, 43
African missionary associates, 48
African mission historiography, 17
African perspectives, 27
African primal religion, 18
African proverbs, 18
African religion, 18, 124
African religious consciousness, 18

INDEX

Africans, 17, 19, 25, 29, 33, 37, 78, 89, 102, 122
   authentically, 102
   depicted, 18
African Safari for Jesus, 106, 138
African traditional religions, 23, 43
African voices, 18
African worldviews, 18
Agbo Areg, 137
Agboola, David T., 27, 29, 36–37, 96, 107, 123, 137
age, golden, 9, 24
agency, 18–19, 27
   foreign, 15
   grassroots, 14
   indigenous, 4
   local, x, 14
agenda, 75, 78
   historical, ix
   revisionist, 15
agents, 50, 106
Agharaumuna, Solomon O., 40, 90
A.H.A., 53, 55, 138
Ahoada Hospital in Nigeria, 107, 140
Ajayi, J. F. Ade, 19, 48, 137
Ajibade, 109–11, 114–15
Ajide, 115, 129, 137
Aladura, 90
Alalade, 27, 29, 36, 70, 137
Alao, 35–36, 82, 96, 137
alcohol, 121
Alexander, C. W., 55
Alignment, 9–10
all-night prayers, 110–11, 113–15, 128
Amalgamation Report, 51
American Adventism, 74
American Adventist missionary, 29
American Adventists, 130
American Christian Missions, 98, 139
American doctor, 106
Amo languages, 42, 67

Andrews University, 137–38, 144, 146
Andross, E. E., 31, 143
Annual Division Meeting, 45, 138
Annual Statistical Report, 28, 137
Anonaba, 38, 137
Anosike, Luke U., 27, 29, 138
anthropological approaches, 15, 19
Apostolic Church, 91
application, 52, 60–66, 131
archival, 2–3
Archives, 102, 137
area, xi, 29, 41, 43, 46, 56, 59, 64–65, 67, 95, 119, 123, 133
Arewa House Archives, 53, 55, 138
arrival, x, 29, 57, 61, 121
articles, ix, 2–3, 47
ASF (Adventist Student Fellowships), 108
Ashton, Ernest, 37
Asia, 12, 14
assessment, 18, 138
Assessment of the Impact, 108, 110, 114–16
ASWA, 113, 140
attribute, 24, 42, 101
Australasian Record and Advent World Survey, 144, 146
authorities, 53–55, 65, 78, 99
Ayandele, E. A., 19, 138
Ayandele, E. O., 51
Ayodeji Abodunde, 95
Azubuike, 22

Baale, 36
Babalola, 81, 108, 110–11, 114–16
   David O., 111, 113–14, 138
   James A. O., 113–15, 138
Babatunde, S. O., 108, 138
Babcock, x, 29, 32, 35–37, 42, 45, 122
   David C., x, 29–30, 32, 34–36, 45, 48, 73, 122, 138
   Elder D. C., 31
Babcock team, 36, 45, 73

INDEX

Babcock University (BU), 29, 128
Bachelor, 109
Background to Nationalism, 139, 144
Ban, 141
  supposed, 115
Baptism, 36, 42, 73, 83–84, 113
Barnes, Andrew E., 50–51, 53–57,
  59, 138
Barriers
  cultural, 133
  linguistic, 93
  religious, 72
Bartlett, 88, 90
  C. A., 40, 87
  W. T., 138
Bassey, Magnus O., 61, 68, 138
Battle Creek College, 35
Bauman, Herman, 106, 138
Baur, John, 48, 95, 138
Bediako, 18, 138
beginnings of indigenization, 2,
  94–119, 147
Beliefs, 15, 22, 81, 110, 122, 125, 135
  core, 130
Believers, 12, 73, 88, 108, 110, 129
bells, 52, 91, 102
  cathedral, 88
from below, 20, 104
benevolent spirits, 89, 126
Benin, 47
Benin City Nigeria, 48, 146
Benin Kingdom, 47, 72
Benne River teaching school, 32
Benue, 57, 61
Benue Province, 56
Berkeley, 139
Berlin, 141, 143
Berrien Springs, 141
Biafra, 103, 104, 105, 106, 112, 146
Biafran Adventists, 105
Biafran War, 107, 111
Bible, 24, 32–33, 38, 53, 91, 105,
  108, 125, 131
Bible studies, 32, 121, 123

Bible study classes, 74
biblical day, 33
Birnin Gwari, 65
Black missionaries, 53–54
Blantyre, 141
Bonny, 32–33, 73
Born-again awakening, 113, 128
Bosch, David J., 24, 70, 138
Bracknell, 146–47
Bradshaw, Mina, 35
Branson, William H., 84
Brass people, 33
Brass Tribe, 81
Brief History, 39–40, 74, 87, 90, 97,
  105–6, 125, 142
Brill, 2, 141
Britain, 48
British, 49, 79
British administration, 52
British Adventist missionary, 29
British Advent Messenger, 143
British authorities, 51, 59
British colonial administration,
  33–34, 48, 50, 72, 75, 78
British decolonization, xi
British Empire, 72, 97
British Guiana Mission, 35, 45
British West Africa, 78
BU (Babcock University), 29, 128
Bukola (Bukky) Ajide, 115, 129, 137
Bulus Y., 140
Burgess, Richard, 91, 95, 103–4,
  111–12, 138

caffeine, 121
Calabar, 79, 124
Cameron, 56, 59
  Donald, 55
Campbell, 82
  Malcolm N., 82, 138
  Michael W., 147
Camp meetings, 38–39, 123
Camp-Meetings in Southern
  Nigeria, 81, 139

153

INDEX

campus, 111, 113, 116, 128
   public, 108, 111, 113
campus revivals, 4, 27, 94–96, 107–8, 110–11, 115, 117–18, 127–29
campus worship services, 114
Canadian Union Messenger, 89
Cannibals, 41
Casa Publicadora Brasileira, 141
cases, 30–31, 49, 58, 69, 72, 77, 81–82, 84–86, 93, 95, 117, 121–22, 125, 139–40
   polygamous, 83
case studies, 71, 75, 95, 144
Cass, Frank, 139, 143
Catholic influence, 48
Catholicism, 71
Catholics, 28, 121
Centuries, 9, 23, 47–49, 71–72, 146
Charismatic Movement in Nigeria, 113, 144
Charismatic movements, 39, 87, 114–15, 138, 144
Charismatic Movements in Modern Nigeria, 144
Charismatic practices, 114, 128
Charismatic renewal, 89, 125–26
   indigenous, 93
charismatic tendencies, 71, 95, 125
charismatism, 69
charismatization, 127
Chicago, 146
chieftaincies, 49
Chigemezi N., 147
Chikelu I., 140
China, 143
Chinese Adventists, 14
Chow, Christie, 14, 138
Christ, 2, 5, 8–9, 22, 32, 69–70, 80–81, 121, 147
   Jesus, 122
   return of, 70, 81, 121
Christian, L. H., 138

Christianity, 33, 48, 50, 52–53, 70, 84, 95, 97, 104, 123, 131, 133, 142
   born-again, 104
   global, 18, 28, 131, 145
   indigenous, 119
Christianity in Africa, 18, 48, 138, 146
Christianity in Nigeria, 47, 50, 91, 95, 97, 137, 140
Christianity in Northern Nigeria, 56, 139
Christianity in West Africa, 56, 142
Christianization, 48, 77–78
Christian missionaries, 44, 48, 50–56, 68, 75, 98, 125, 143, 144
Christian missionary scene in Nigeria, 44, 46
Christian mission history, 95
Christian missions, 48–49, 51–52, 54, 56, 70, 75, 79, 95–98, 140–41, 145
   earliest, 29, 71
Christian Missions/Establishment, 53, 143
Christian Missions in Nigeria, 19, 68, 137
Christian movement, indigenous, 98
Christian Origins in Muslim, 145
Christian Remnant, 70, 141
Christians, 28, 45, 50–52, 54, 59, 78, 91, 98, 107, 118, 124
Christie, 14
Christocentric, 18
Christ Seventh Day, 81
Christ's parousia, 69, 80, 95
Christ's return, ix, 7, 9, 21, 22–23, 95
chronological surveys, 11
chronology, 3, 20
Chucks, J. O., 107, 139
Church, 3–4, 9–11, 13–14, 18–19, 24, 39–40, 48, 73–75, 81–86, 104, 107–8, 115–17, 126–27, 130–31, 135

INDEX

indigenous, 10, 79
indigenous Adventist, 98
local Adventist, 114, 124
mainline, 104
remnant, ix, 23
worldwide, 16
young, 134
Civil, 94
civilization, 70
civilizers, 19
civil war, 2, 4, 26–27, 94, 96, 102–3, 105, 117–18, 131, 147
destructive, xi
The Civil War Revival and Its Pentecostal Progeny, 138
Clarendon, 141
Clarke, C. A. N., 57, 65
Clarke, C. N. A., 139
Clifford, 29, 34–35, 38–40, 80–83, 85–86, 145
Hugh, 103
Jesse C., x, 29, 33–34, 38, 45, 73, 78, 100, 116, 124, 139
Ukwu, 116
Winnie D., 38
Clifford University, 29
CMS, 48, 51, 54, 56
CMS missionaries, 51
Coleman, 72
James, 139
college, 97
Colonel Odumegwu Ojukwu, 103
Colonial administrators, 51–54, 58, 138
Colonial authorities, 15, 27, 47, 51–53, 68, 79
local, 52
Colonial authorities' plans, 78
Colonial-era failures, 19
Colonial governmental policies, 49
Colonialism, 70, 75, 97, 122, 145
Colonial masters, 15, 97
Colonial mission structure, 15
Colonial Northern Nigeria, 139–40

Colonial officers, 53
Colonial policies, 4, 49, 68, 79
Colonial politics, 2, 44, 49, 68, 144
Colonial regime, 79
Colonial structures, 4, 80
Colonies, 53
supervise, 49
colonization, 49, 72
Colorado, 30
Colorado Conference, 30
colored man, 31
colporteur work, 31
Columbian Union Visitor, 146
Come, 1, 23–24, 33, 41, 50, 52, 87, 107, 145
Comity agreements, xi
Commissioned laymen, 30, 45, 72
Communal lives, 89, 126
Communities, 11, 17–18, 20, 37, 42, 67, 127
Competition, 61, 128
Complexities, 16, 75, 83
Compounds, 39, 123
Concept, 3, 12, 21–22, 24–25, 56
Conception, 1, 77, 95
Conception stage, 2
Conference, 35, 56
local, 110–11
Conference, Virginia, 35
confessional, 3, 20
Conflict, 21, 26, 59, 69–70, 95, 116
context, ix, 4–5, 7, 71, 90, 104, 126, 128, 134–35
cultural, 135
economic, 132
historical, x
local, 24, 133
sociopolitical, 17
socioreligious, 120
unique cultural and religious, 121, 135
Contextualization, 13, 16, 71, 146
cultural, x
Contextualized Mission History, 120

INDEX

contextualizes, 5, 120
Continent, 9, 15–16, 97, 141
continuities, 18, 24, 115
Contours of European Adventism, 13, 141
Contribution, 29, 70, 92, 98
Controversy, 109
conversations, 17, 95, 99
conversion, 43, 87–88, 122–26
convictions, 33, 70, 82, 110, 146
Cookey, 21, 139
Coon, Roger W., 101, 139
cooperation, 50, 132
Cordelia, 83, 85–86
Cormack, A. W., 82, 139
Correspondences, 143, 145
corruption, 19, 112, 126
cosmos, 89, 126
Council, 57–58
Council Action, 84–85, 140
Council of Missions, 57–58
counterfeit, 88, 93
country, x, 10, 14, 24, 30, 32, 58, 96, 102–5, 112, 120–22, 135
Crampton, E. P. T., 56, 139
Crisis, 26, 89, 116, 119, 121, 130–32, 142
The Crisis of Religious Politics and Secular, 140
Culture, 9, 18, 70–71, 75, 77, 81, 86, 91–92, 95, 100, 121–22, 127, 143
  denominational, 126, 133
Curse of Africa, 82
Customs, 76, 82, 86, 124
  local, 4, 85
Damsteegt, P. Gerard, 10–11, 24, 139
Daniells, Arthur G., 9
Danmole, H. O., 50, 139
Dauphin, R. P., 29, 35, 45, 73
Daystar, 137, 142
Decision, 4, 45, 54, 62, 64, 82–84, 109, 116
  contingent, 12

local, 13
Dede, C. H., 39
Deeper Life Christian Ministry, 112, 127
Denmark, 113
Denomination, 8–9, 15, 43, 72, 90, 98–99, 101, 105, 107–8, 117, 127, 129–30, 141
  premillennialist, 119
Denominationalism, 146
Denomination-ally, 21, 108
Denominational mission, 73
Denominational publications, 25
Denominational structures, 13
Departure, 93, 95
Devastation, 26, 96
Development
  educational, 26
  health, 124
  historical, 20
Development of Adventist Missiology, 9, 12, 141
Diara, Benjamin C., 98, 139
dichotomization, 124, 126, 131
Dick, E. D., 41, 139
Dickay, Albert J., 101
dietary rules, 106
Dike, A. J., 38
Dinneya, 38
Dioka, J., 77, 139
Director, 37, 39, 45, 57, 65–66, 102, 113
  assistant publishing, 110–11
direct proselytization, 4
disagreements, 40, 91
Disappointment, 8
discourse, 70, 96, 120, 132
diseases, 89, 106
disengagement, 69
  cultural, 92
Disgrace, 83–84
Disillusionment, 103
Dispensary, 41, 60, 64, 67, 123
Disruptive civil war, xi

Dissatisfaction, 109, 129
Dissenters, 97
Dissertation, 96, 113–14
Distances, 41, 47, 72
Distinctive history, 120, 135
Distinctives, 12
Distribution, 130, 145
District, 63–64, 80
District, Jere, 67
district officer, 60–61, 79, 142
Districts, Ron, 59
diversity, 10, 132–33
    cultural, 92
    ethnic, 103
divination, 89, 125–26
divine, 19, 104
divine initiative, 24–25
divine momentum, 25
Divine Power, 101
Divisions, ix, 15, 56, 102–3, 137
Divorce, 83, 146
Doctrines, 4, 13, 91, 104, 135
Dodds, William, 19, 139

Early Adventism, 122
Early Adventist Mission, 13, 145
East Africa, xi
East African encounter, 93
Eastern region, 103
Eastern Tidings, 139
East Nigerian Mission, 101
Ecclesial practices, 132
Ecumenical approach, 3, 20
Ecumenical Initiatives, 140
Edmond, L., 39
Education, 8, 15, 35, 37, 74–76, 79, 98, 108, 122, 140
    adult, 42, 68
    formal, 122–23
    physical, 77
Educational Expansion, 61, 68, 138
educational feat, 37
educational functions, 78
educational programs, 38, 50

educational work, 38
education sector, 112
Eerdmans, 139
Effectiveness, 12, 67
Efforts
    communal, 75
    indigenous, 43
    pioneering, 14–15
    supported evangelistic, 74
    trailblazing, 26
Egharevba, Jacob, 47, 139
Ekechi, Felix K., 61, 68, 139
elections, 101, 103
Elele, 39
elite
    middle-class, 113
    young, 113
Ellen, G., 146
Elmstrom, G. L., 101
Elmstrom, G.M., 143
Emii, 106
Emirate Division, 60, 142
emirates, 55–56, 58
emirs, 52, 55, 59–60
    local, 46
Empire, 54
Enahoro, Anthony, 98
enchantment, 76
enculturation, 11
Encyclopedia of Seventh-day Adventism, 11
Encyclopedia of Seventh-day Adventists, x, 1, 137
end-time, 39, 125, 130
The End-Time Army, 113, 144
Engagement, 88, 92–93, 132
    cultural, 4, 81, 142
England, 57, 59, 62, 75–76, 78
English officials, 64
Epistemological motif, 23
Epistemology, 23–24
    cultural, 22
Epworth, 139
equality, 98, 127

INDEX

era, 9, 11, 14–16, 22, 102
   colonial, 15, 37
   institutionalization, 15
   mission story, 14
   open-door, 8
   transitional, 12
Eregare, Emmanuel Orihentare, 29, 140
Erunmu, 36
   stations of, 37, 122
Erupted, 78, 103
Eschatological hope, 18
Eschatological Remnant, 145
Eschatology, 81
   appropriating Adventist, 129
ESDA, 1–2, 11
Establishment, 11, 14–15, 22, 37, 43, 46–47, 51, 58–59, 66–67, 107, 143–44
   stations,' 67
Ethnocentrism, 77
Ethnographical monograph documents, 14
Ethnography, 3
Ethos, religio-cultural, 78
Eurocentric, 19, 93
   Eurocentric histories, x
   Eurocentric lenses, 26
Europa, 141
Europe, 1, 13–14, 133
European Adventist archives, 2
European Adventist Society, 2
European Christian Missions, 98, 139
Eva, 107
   Duncan W., 140
Evangelism, 15, 109, 122, 132, 144
Evangelistic meetings, 32, 39, 107
Evangelists, 36–38, 59, 63, 107
   literature, 109
   local, 24, 123
Evangelization, 50–51, 53–55, 57, 59, 88, 138
Evil forces, 90, 126
Evil spirits, 87–88

Evo, Josiah, 38
Evoh, Josiah, 39
expansion, 7, 13–15, 61, 67, 112
   denominational, 19
   emphasized geographical, 26
   global Adventist mission, 12
   postwar, 10
Experience, ix, 60, 66, 89, 104, 112–13
   personal, 127
   personal spiritual, 127
Experiences and Convictions, 34, 89
Ezeigbo, Theodora Akachi, 75, 140
Ezenwafor-Afuecheta, 21, 140

Faith, 4, 8, 11, 24–25, 34, 54, 81, 104, 106, 111, 120–21, 131, 134
   apocalyptic, 104
   enculturated, 130
   lived, 19
   newfound, 109
Faith Tabernacle Church, 90
Falola, 49, 51, 72, 79, 103, 140
Farrant, H. G., 56
Father, 34, 82–83, 85, 106
The Fat Lady and the Kingdom, 74, 142
Fattening, 76–77
The Fattening Rite of Passage, 76
Faught, C. Brad, 50, 140
fellowship, 82, 115, 138
Fiedler, 70, 140
Filibus, 42, 67
First Camp-Meeting, 39, 143
flogged, 40, 87, 125
flow, 3, 7, 16–17, 21, 26, 142
fluid, 43
Fly, James L., 113, 140
Foreign Mission Board, 30, 140
foreign transplant, 18
forest, 104
forgiveness, 40, 87, 125
form, 3, 71–72, 78, 86, 124, 128, 133
formal church sanction, 4

INDEX

From the End of the World, 7, 10, 141
Fulani Muslims, 50
Fulani territories, 50
furlough, 78, 80
furniture, 37, 123
further explorations, 26, 86
further studies, 115, 128
future, 3, 5, 8, 18, 20–24, 27, 120–21, 131, 133, 135
future is brighter, ix, 3, 17, 20–21
future of Adventism in Nigeria, 121–35
futuristic projections, 131
Fyfe, Christopher, 18, 146

Galadima, 50, 97, 140
galvanized corrupt system, 126
gap, 116
Gaskiya, 139
GC. *See* General Conference
GC committee, 31
gender issues, 131
General Adventist Mission Historiography, 7
General Conference (GC), 8, 22, 31, 84, 102, 133, 137, 140–41, 143, 145
General Conference Archives, 2, 82, 84, 140, 145
General Conference Committee, 31, 34, 140
General Conference Corporation, 60
General Conference Department, 35, 140
General Conference Headquarters, 84
General Conference President Robert H. Pierson, 102
General Conference Radio Secretary, 101
General Conference Radio Secretary Tours Nigeria, 139

General Conference Session, 82, 102
General Conference Session Action, 82, 145
General Yakubu Gowon, 103
Generation, 128
   younger, 111, 135
Ghana, x, 30–31, 33, 35–36, 38, 40, 45, 73, 81, 109, 139
   entered, 30
Ghanaian Adventist, 73
Gifford, Paul, 144
Global homogeneity, 133
Globalization, 132
Global North, 16
Global South Christianity, 131
Glocal, 132
Glocality, 132–33
God, 7–8, 19, 22–25, 40–41, 43, 87–90, 99–100, 106, 108–10, 117, 127, 130
   bless, 33
   movement of, 24, 26
   power of, 89, 126
God Church, 91
Godfrey Harold, 141
God's kingdom, 22, 106
God's Providence, 106, 142
God-talk, 134
Gold Coast, 32–33, 35, 141
Golden jubilee, 107, 137
Gombe, 56
Gospel, 8, 22, 37, 43, 134
Gottfried, 144
Gottfried Oosterwal, 9
Göttingen, 141
government, 29, 52, 54–55, 99–100, 112, 126
   colonial, xi, 33, 44, 53–55, 73
   federal, 103
   government officials, 55
   government schoolmaster, 33
   government schools, 34, 38–39
   government service, 38

159

INDEX

government (continued)
   governor, 54–55, 72, 103
   lieutenant, 64
   military, 103, 107
Grain, 81, 139
Gramlich, John, 28, 141
Grand Rapids, 139
Grassroots level, 133
Grassroots networks, 14
Great Disappointment, 7–8, 11
Greenleaf, Floyd, 13, 141
Groundwork of the Seventh-day Adventist Church History in Nigeria, 140
Group, 8, 34, 39–40, 45, 73, 81, 87, 111–13, 117, 123–24, 128–29
   anti-missionary, 55
   ethnic, 71, 103
   religious, 124
group process, 125
growth, 13–14, 16, 23, 25, 45–46, 73–74, 96, 103, 127, 132, 144
   economic, 112
   institutional, 14
   organizational, 15
   phenomenal, 16

Hackett, Rosalind I. J., 124, 141
Hagiographical narratives, 14
Hale, Dudley, 32–33, 141
Hallucinations, 125
Hamilton, 36
   James J., 35–36, 42, 45, 73
Handover, 15, 97
Hardships, 22, 61, 122
Harold, 25
Hartlapp, Johannes, 13, 141
harvest, 24, 135
Hastings, 48, 95, 141
   Adrian, 95
Hausa, 36, 42, 50, 67
Hausa-Fulani, 72
Hausa languages, 53
Hausa man, 67

Hausa Nigerians, 122
Hausa regions, 48
Hayford, 32–34, 43
   J. D., 32–33
   Sydney, x, 29–30, 32–34, 42, 73
headquarters, 56, 64, 108, 116–17
   administrative, 105
   conference, 109
Healing, 87–88, 104
   Miraculous, 89
Healing ministries, 16
Healing prophet, 90
Health, 31, 74, 113
Healthcare, 15
Healthcare systems, 121
Health facilities, 92, 105–6
Healthful living, 122
Health Station, 58
Healthy lifestyle, 121
Heart, 3, 25, 41, 80
Hearts of Faith, 11–12, 146
Heathen, 76–77
Heathen Igbo women, 86
Heaton, Matthew M., 49, 51, 72, 79, 103, 140
Heaven, 22, 121
Heinz, Daniel, 1, 13, 141, 146
Herald, 138, 141, 144–45
Heritage, 43, 118–19
   indigenous religious, 19
A Heritage of Faith, 95, 137
Herman-Hodge, H., 54
Hermeneutic, 25, 43, 129
Heterogeneity, 133
Historians, 8, 23–24, 36
   indigenous, 15
   professionally trained, 9
historical accounts, 2, 9, 21, 27, 43
Historical data, 2–3, 29, 89, 100
Historical narratives, 8, 11, 21
   potent, 3, 20
Historiographical reflection, 1, 16, 25
Historiography, x, 7, 10, 13, 17, 20–21, 25–26

INDEX

ecumenical, 18
identity-confirming, 12
institutional, 19
interdisciplinary, 9
triumphalist, 10-11
History, ix-x, 2-3, 5, 7-9, 11-13, 17-18, 20-21, 23, 43, 72, 74-75, 105, 141-42, 144
comprehensive institutional, 13
missiological, 14
religious, 11
secular, 9
unique, 120, 131, 135
history foregrounds, 20
History in Missiological Perspective, 14, 146
A History of Benin, 47, 139
History of Christianity, 72, 95-96, 98
History of Christianity in Africa, 29, 48, 142
History of Nigeria, 49, 51, 72, 79, 95, 103, 140
Holy Spirit, 39, 87-90, 112-13, 125-27
Homes, 31, 33, 76, 79, 85, 115
Honors, 20, 29
Hoornaert, Eduardo, 18
Höschele, Stefan, 1, 7, 10, 12-13, 58, 70, 84, 93, 141
Hospitals, 13, 25, 60-61, 64, 74, 105, 107
House fellowships, 115
Houses, 41, 60, 78, 80
thatch, 39, 123
Humanity, 92, 106
Hunger, 105-6
Husbands, 77, 83
Hyatt, 30-32, 34, 42, 45, 73
James M., x, 29-31, 34, 42, 45, 73, 141
Marian, 30-31
Hyde, J. A., 29, 35, 40-42, 46, 58, 60, 62, 64-65, 67-68, 99, 123
Hyde, J. J., 141

Hyde, John J., 29, 40, 42, 46, 57
Hyde, John J. N. A. K. Zar., 141
Hyde, L. M. Fieldwork, 142
Hyde, Louisa, 41, 123

Ibadan, 36, 41, 45-46, 60, 66, 73-74, 90, 97, 108-9, 112-13, 137-39, 141-42
Ibadan army, 48
Ibadan University Press, 139
Ibo Country, 76-77, 83, 85, 146
Ibo Opening, 19, 139
Ibo Traditional Religion, 89, 142
Ibo Women, 144
Identity, 11, 119, 130-32
cultural, 23
denominational, 14, 117
distinct theological, 20
functional, 117, 130
national, 13, 103
primary, 117
Identity crisis, 16, 131-33, 135
Ideologies
policing/enforcing Adventist, 124
religious, 122
Ife, 72, 108, 110, 112, 142
Ifeka J. Onyeocha, 140
Igbo Adventists, 94, 104, 106, 116-18, 126
young male, 104
Igbo casualties, 103
Igbo children, 21
Igbo concept, 3, 20
Igbo Female Writer, 140
The Igbo in Perspective, 139
Igbo kingdoms, 72
Igboland, 39, 48, 79, 91, 123, 139, 144
Igbo language, 17, 39
Igbo man, 105
Igbo market women, 79
Igbo Marriage, 77, 144
Igbo name, 1
Igbo native law, 82
Igbo phrase, 21

INDEX

Igbo religious landscape, 103
Igbos, 1, 21, 23, 39, 43, 46, 75, 103–7, 116, 122–24
Igbo society, 104, 139–40
Igbo Studies Association, 142
Igbo term, ix
Igbo tradition, 76
Igbo wisdom, 22
Igbo women, 75, 78
Igbo Women's War, 146
Igbo worldview, 24, 126
Igwe, 22, 142
Igwebuike, 144
Ihie, 97, 105–6
Ijebu, 72
Ile-Ife Hospital, 74
Ilishan-Remo, 97
illness, 31, 37
Ilogu, Edmund, 89, 142
Ilorin, 37, 46, 48, 51, 54, 122
imminence, 69, 80, 100
Independence, 2, 15, 27, 94, 96–98, 100–103, 118, 147
   political, 95–96
   religious, 94, 98, 117–18
Independence era, 117
Independent states, 49, 72
Indigenes, 34, 37, 125
Indigenization, xi, 4, 96–97, 118
Indigenization process, 94
Indigenizing, 40, 90
Indigenous Charismatics, 86
indigenous cultures, 13, 27, 69–70, 92, 124
Indigenous Encounters, 125, 143
Indigenous initiatives, 14, 25
Indigenous issues, 26, 69–70, 74, 95
Indigenous issues in Nigeria, 2, 71–93, 147
Indigenous layman, 45
Indigenous leaders, 4, 15
Indigenous life, lived realties of, 90, 126
Indigenous pastors, 98

Indigenous peoples, 125
Indigenous power structures, 49
Indigenous practices, 75
Indigenous Reclamation, 27
Indirect rule, 49–52, 140
Individuals, 12, 107, 127
Inevitable Appeal, 101, 143
Inheritance, 15, 82–83
Initiated churches, 28
Initiative, foreign, 25
Innovation, 15, 91, 128, 131
Institute, 33, 141
Institutionalization, 14–15
Institutional mission approaches, 93
Institutional organizations, 73, 92
Institutions, 26, 73–75, 97, 107
   educational, 37–38, 122
   healthcare, 122
   most difficult, 82
   printing, 74
Instruments, 111, 116, 144
   local, 111
Integration, 3, 20
Intention, 46, 62, 66
Interaction, complex, 93
Interchurch Relations, 58, 141
Interdenominational interactions, 20
Interdenominational relations, 3
Interference, 52–53, 56, 64
International Missionary Council, 55, 57
International Review of Mission, 142
Interpretations, xi, 131
   postmodern world, 131
Interpreters, 38
Interpretive frameworks, 16, 26
interview, 40, 57–58, 90, 105, 109–11, 114, 116, 128, 138
   oral, 3, 96
Invisibility, 146
Ipoti-Ekiti, 36–37, 122
Iru-mgbede, 76–77
Isichei, Elizabeth, 29, 48, 72, 95–96, 98, 142

INDEX

Ising, Walter K., 46, 142
Islam, 48, 50, 52, 54, 137
Islamic religion, 50, 52
Itinerating in Nigeria, 36, 39, 143, 145
Itinerating in Southern Nigeria, 39, 145
Iwuchukwu, Marinus C., 50–52, 142
Izima, David A., 39–40, 74, 87, 90, 97, 105–6, 125, 142

Jamaica, 13, 145
James, 30
Japan, 14, 146
Jean-Henri Merle d'Aubigné, 9
Jengre, 40–41, 46, 67, 123
Jenkins, Philip, 131
Jesse, 81, 145
Jesus, 81
Jewelry, 121
Jigger, 67
Jigger flea, 41, 123
Jihad conquests, 48
John, 40, 123
John Garah Nengel, 2
Joint Church, 138
Jones, Alonzo T., 8
Jones, A. T., 9, 86
Jos, 2, 40, 47, 54, 57, 59, 65–67
Jos Division, 66–67
Joseph Adeyemo Adeogun, 101
Joseph Ayo Babalola, 90
Jos-Zaria road, 59
juju priests, 87, 124
justice, 18, 22, 127

Kabwir, 52
Kachia, 59, 65
Kaduna, 47, 53, 56, 58, 138, 144
Kaji Dariya, 67
Kakwi, 67
 sons of, 42, 67
Kalu, Ogbu U., x, 3, 17–20, 25, 56, 142
Kaplan, Steven, 70, 77–78, 84, 142

Katab people, 62–63
Katab tribe, 63
Katuka, 61
Kauru, 65
Kenneth, 145
Kern, M. E., 36, 142
Kingdom, 47, 49, 69, 71–72, 92, 100, 117, 129
 supernatural, 95
 west-central Africa, 71
Kingdom Integration, 81, 92, 100, 142
Kingsley Chukwuemeka, 137
Knight, George R., 9–10, 73–74, 142
Kofi, 145
Kolade, J. O. Y., 108, 142
Krum, Ronald E., 106, 142
Kuranga, Abraham A., 27, 29, 70, 96–98, 101, 111, 142
Kurmin Musa, 63
Kwame Bediako, 18
Kwara State, 46

Lagos, 31–32, 36, 115–16, 129, 137–38, 140, 144
Lake Union Herald, 89
Lamba, 42, 67
Lamin Sanneh, 19, 145
Langer, 81, 92, 100
 Richard C., 142
 Rick, 81
Langford, L. F., 31, 34, 37, 143
language, 4, 63, 134
 local, 37
Lanham, 139
lantern slides, 38
Las G., 144
Lashier, S. J., 46, 142
Latecomers, 28, 46–47, 49, 92
Lateness, 29, 68, 71
Latin America, 13
The latter rain, 39, 87
Lawson, Ronald, 116, 142
Laymen, 30, 98

Laypeople, 34, 99, 118
Laypersons, 101
Leaders, 5, 9, 39, 46, 80, 83–84, 87, 90, 109, 112, 115, 129, 135
Leadership, 13, 16, 38, 51, 97, 110–11, 113–14, 118, 128
   conference, 111
   denominational, 113
   foreign, 94
   indigenous, 96, 101–2
   local, 107, 118
   local Adventist, 110
   national, 98
Lecture, 40, 87–88
Leitmotif, 3
Lekki, 137
Levitical laws, 121
Liberia, 31, 36
licentiates, 30–31, 35
lieutenant-governor, 54–55
Life Sketches, 5, 146
Light Shines, 108
Limiting Factors, 27, 29, 36, 70, 96, 137
Lindenfeld, David, 125, 143
Lindstrom, P. R., 107
Linnel, Irving N., 31, 143
Liturgy, 110, 116, 129
Lived realities, 22, 124
Livelihoods, 98, 100
Lizards, 106
Localization, 96, 118
Local leaders, 4, 13
Local mission, 101
Local Mission officers, 108
Local natives, 61
Local particularity, 132
Local pastors, 35, 100–101, 107
Lokoja, 32, 56
London, 54–55, 59, 137–39, 142–43
Longman, 137–38
looted factories, 79
Ludwig Richard Conradi, 13, 35, 141

Lugard, 48, 50–52, 59
   Frederick D., 143
   Lord Frederick D., 5, 64, 88, 72, 110
Lutheran Church, 56
Luviri, 140

Maigadi, Ibrahim B., 27, 29, 41–42, 67, 96, 143
Malawi, 30, 140
Malevolent spirits, 89, 126
Mallam Lamba Kakwi, 67
Manifestations, 39–40, 84, 87, 90
Marcauley, Herbert, 98
Marou, Henri, 18
Marriage, 76–77, 83, 85, 139, 146
Marriage in Igboland, 77, 139
Marrou, Henri, 18
Maryknoll, 138, 145–46
Maryland, xi, 82, 84, 140
Masfa, Gabriel, ix, 11, 15–16, 131, 143
Maxwell, 71, 82
   A. S., 143
Mayang, 42, 67
Mbaise, 105
Mbano, 105
McAdams, Daniel, 9
McClements, William, 34, 36–37, 39, 41, 45–46, 57, 59, 61–66, 76, 82, 86–88, 123
Medical Institutions of the Seventh-day Adventist in Southeastern Nigeria, 144
Medical items, 105
Medical missions, 26, 32, 57–59, 63–64, 123
Medical Missions Approach, 146
Medical work, 41–42, 50, 62, 64, 123
Medicine, 41
Meetings, 54–56, 65, 99, 109
   private prayer, 112
   stakeholders,' 58
   workers,' 40, 87, 99, 114–15

INDEX

Members, 28, 36, 48, 52, 74, 76, 79,
    85–86, 90, 98, 108, 116, 128
  foundational, 82, 124
  losing, 128
  probationary, 84–85
Membership Statistics, 137
Memorandum, 59, 144
Memorialists, 52
memory
  historical, 18
  institutional, 3, 17, 20
men
  educated, 51, 76
  helping, 79
Mennonite Brethren, 51
metamorphosed, 127
metaphor, 22, 25
Miller, Walter, 51
Millerites, 7–8
minister, 33, 35, 38, 73, 101
  commissioned, 30, 35
ministerial directory, 31
ministry, 31, 38, 110, 142
  blessed, 113
  pastoral, 89
  vibrant music, 32
Missiology, x, 139, 141
  comparative, 12
  open-door, 8
Mission, 7–12, 18, 22–26, 36–41,
    43–46, 51, 55–60, 62–64,
    66–68, 72–73, 75–76,
    92–93, 97, 121, 123
Mission activities, 57–58, 68
  evangelistic, 74
Missionaries, ix–x, 13–16, 26,
    29–30, 36–37, 44–45, 47,
    49–51, 53–58, 61, 68–72,
    77–78, 80, 84–85, 92–93,
    98, 101, 117–18, 121–22,
    124–26
  commissioned, 30, 35, 45, 73
  denominational, 121
  early, 37, 116
  forced, 4
  foreign, 25, 97
  group of, 36, 122
  medical, 105
  pioneer, 29, 33, 100
  pioneer Advent, 42
  portraying, 19
  seasoned, 35
  self-supporting, 30, 45, 72
  sixteenth-century Catholic, 29
Missionary Adventism, 74, 98, 107,
    115, 117–18, 126, 130–31
Missionary Enterprise and Rivalry
    in Igboland, 61, 68, 139
Missionary Era, 142
The Missionary Impact on Modern
    Nigeria, 19, 138
Missionary Rivalry, 2, 44, 61, 68,
    138, 144
Missionary Worker, 138–39
Mission board, xi, 24, 62–63
Mission bodies, 44, 58, 68, 118
Mission fields, 9, 38, 74, 76, 81, 99,
    101
Mission group, 68
Mission headquarters, 46
Mission historians, 5, 12, 16–17,
    23, 25
Mission history, 3, 8, 12–13, 20,
    22–23, 25, 43, 70, 93
Missionizing, 55–56
  contextual, 132, 134
Mission leaders, 40, 90, 126
Mission Problem, 146
Mission rivalry, 57, 61, 68
Mission schools, 25, 32
Mission station, 36–37, 41, 46, 54,
    59, 67–68
Mission work, 26, 29–30, 37, 40–41,
    46, 67, 69–70, 73, 86, 88, 95
Mitchison, Lois, 85, 143
Models, 4, 12, 19, 132, 144
  historiographical, 11
  questioned inherited mission, 13

INDEX

Mohammedan religion, 52
momentum, 13, 40, 87
   institutional, 12
Monsell, C. N. M., 57, 59, 139, 143
Morgue, Samuel D., 29, 35–37,
   45, 73
Motus Dei, 24–26, 141
Movement, 25, 37, 40, 87–90, 115,
   124–29
   charismatic-Pentecostal, 115
   divine, 25
   evangelical, 10
   grassroots, 24
   holistic, 74
   indigenous, 90
   nationalist, 97
   political freedom, 99
Multiple religious belonging, 122,
   124, 131
Multi-voice lenses, 10
Muri Province, 56
Music, 116, 128
   indigenous, 116
Muslim-Adventist relations, 131
Muslim areas, 52, 55, 59
Muslim-Christian Dialogue, 50–52
Muslim-dominated regions, 59
Muslim inhabitants, 46
Muslim North, 51, 55
   colonial, 57
Muslim regions, 46, 54
Muslim rulers, 50
Muslims, 41, 50, 53, 123
Muslim sources, 47
Muslim territories, 54
Muslim World, 146
Mustard Seed, 81, 137, 139

NAAS (National Association of
   Adventist Students), 108
Nagel, 105
Nairobi, 138, 144
National Association of Adventist
   Students (NAAS), 108

Nationalism, 96
   post-independence, 4
nationalists, 97–99
nationals, 97, 113
Native Assistance, 60
Native Baptist Church, 98
Native Hospital, 58
Nche, George C., 98, 139
NED (Northern European
   Division), 41, 102
Nengel, John G., 2, 44, 144
NEWAD (Northern Europe–West
   Africa Division), 102
Newbold Academic, 146–47
New Branch Sabbath School, 107,
   139
New Dimension in African
   Christianity, 144
New Elite, 137
Newest Nation, 143
New Hampshire, 35
Newmann, 53, 144
New Series, 137
New Song, 71, 146
New York, 142, 145
New York University Press, 142
The Next Christendom, 131
Ngwa Igbos, 39, 123
Ngwa people, 38
Niger, 48, 50
Niger Delta, 33, 71, 81, 83, 124, 139
Niger expedition, 48
Nigeria, ix–xi, 2, 17, 26–49, 68–74,
   88, 90–92, 95–103, 107,
   111–13, 115–24, 126–28,
   130–35, 139–41, 143–45
   colonization of, 49, 72
   governor of, 54–55
   history in, 16
   history of Adventism in, 27, 74,
      86, 95–96
   rocked, 127
Nigeria Mission, 37, 144

INDEX

Nigerian Adventism, ix, 2, 4, 94–95, 102, 117–18, 120, 127–28, 130–35
  glocal nature of, 132–33
  unique, 27, 121
Nigerian Adventists, ix, 27, 36, 98, 117–18, 124–30, 132–34
  younger, 135
Nigerian African metaphysics, 89
Nigerian agency, 26
Nigerian Christianity, 132
Nigerian Christians, 97–98, 115
Nigerian Civil War, 95, 107
Nigerian congregations, 128
Nigerian culture, 95, 118, 122, 124, 132, 135
Nigerian Emirates, 146
Nigerian front, 64, 91, 146
Nigerian metaphysics, 90, 126
Nigerian mission, 35–36, 45, 73
Nigerian missionary arena, 48
Nigerian mission field, 61–62, 68, 143
Nigerian Pentecostalism, 115, 127, 129, 146
Nigerian religious context fertile, 112
Nigerian religious market, 128
Nigerian response, 121, 126
Nigerians, 25, 28, 33, 97, 101, 107, 115, 120, 122, 127, 135
  average, 79
  educated, 51
  indigenous, 83
  local, x
Nigerian Seventh-day Adventist history, ix
Nigerian society, 127
Nigerian socioreligious sphere, 120, 135
Nigerian state, 48, 129
Nigerian story, 118, 142
Nigerian Training College, 97
Nigerian Union, 116

Nigerian Union Mission, 39, 45–46, 63, 110, 113, 143
Nigeria's Christian Revolution, 91, 95, 103–4, 112, 138
Nigeria's National Development, 139
Nigeria Union Mission, 76, 107
Niger Province, 56
Niger River, 48
Njoku, Moses, 105, 144
Nkeiruka, ix, 1–135, 142
Nkpu, 76–77
Nnamdi Azikiwe, 98
Nnoroviele, Salome C., 75, 144
non-Adventists, 2, 108, 121
non-Christian rituals, 111
non-Millerites, 8
non-Muslim minority ethnicities, 52
Non-Western Religion, 138
Nordic missionaries, 111
Normington, L. W., 42, 68
North, 2, 40–42, 44, 46–58, 68, 99, 101, 103, 107, 123
Northeastern Nigerian Mission, 45
Northeast Mission, 46, 57
Northern, 32, 44, 72
northern banks, 57
Northerners, 117
Northern European Division (NED), 41, 102
Northern Europe–West Africa Division (NEWAD), 102
northern leaders, 50–51
Northern Nigeria, 2, 4, 29, 40, 44, 46–47, 49, 52, 54–55, 58, 64, 66, 68, 137–38, 144–45
Northern Nigerian crisis, 23
Northern Protectorates, 48–49, 52
northern provinces, 56, 58, 64
  secretary of, 64
northern towns, 46
North Nigerian Mission, 99
North Pacific Union Gleaner, 142, 147
north perspectives, 12

INDEX

north seemed, 56
Northwestern Nigerian Mission, 45
nostalgia, 17, 23
nostalgic recollections, 3, 20
Notre Dame Press, 138
Nuefeld, Don, 144
Numan, 56
Nupe, 53
Nupeland, 56
Nwadialor, 98, 144
Nwauwa, Apollos O., 139
Nyekwere, David, 38, 144

Obafemi Awolowo, 98
Obafemi Awolowo University, 112
Office, 1, 39, 53, 55, 80, 100, 137
   colonial, 54, 58
   provincial, 62
Officer, 53, 58
   divisional, 59
Official missionary, 34, 45, 73, 122
officials, 62
   colonial, 51
Ogbonna, Daniel, 137
Ojo, 112–13, 115, 127, 144
Oke-Bola, 74, 108–11, 114
Okpualangwa, 105
Olaore, Israel B., 109–11, 113, 115, 128
Oldham, 55, 58
Oliver, 7
   Barry David, 144
Oloyede, 108
Olubukola, David, 115
Onalapo Ajibade, 109, 111, 114
Onwere, Philip, 38–39
Onwuzurigbo, 77, 144
Onyeocha, 21
Onyeodo, 38, 137
Onyeodor, Daniel, 39
Oosterwal, 7, 10, 144
optimism, 22, 81, 103
   eschatological, ix, 3, 21–23
oral accounts, 38

oral histories, 27
Orbis, 138, 145–46
ordinances, 84
ordination, 38
O'Reggio, 13, 145
Orekoya, Daniel, 90
Oriaku, Emmanuel, 106
Orthodoxy, 91
Orthopraxis, 91
Oshogbo, 48
Other Christians, 28, 37, 48, 58, 68, 82, 86, 90, 98, 112, 118
Otun, 97
outlook, 85, 143
   shared, 23
Outlook in Nigeria, 36, 143
Owerri, 79, 106
Owerri Province, 79
Owusu-Mensa, 30, 32, 81, 145
Oxford, 138, 141, 147
The Oxford Handbook of Seventh-day Adventism, 147
Oyeniyi, 36–37, 43, 72
   Bukola A., 140
   Samuel, 36
Oyo, 72
   invading, 48

Pacific, 140, 142, 146
pacifists, 80, 105
pagan, 77, 124
pagan tribes, 51, 53
pain, 22, 100
Pall Mall, 143
Palmer, 55
   E. R., 34
   H. R., 54
palm fronds, 39, 123
Papua New Guinea, xi
Paradigm Shifts in Theology of Mission, 138
Paradise, 59, 145
Parousia, ix, 17, 21–22, 70, 106, 117, 121, 125, 130

INDEX

Passion for Mission, ix, 102, 146–47
Pastors, 35, 40, 87, 106, 115, 118, 129, 133, 143
Paul Yonggi Cho, 115
Pentecost, 39, 87
Pentecostal Adventist church, 129
Pentecostal Adventists, 129
Pentecostal beliefs, 113
Pentecostal born-again practices, 114
Pentecostal Christianity, 127
Pentecostal churches, 127
Pentecostal congregation, 115
Pentecostal experience, 88, 112
Pentecostal Experiences in Nigeria, 87–88
Pentecostal influence, 117
Pentecostalism, 104, 117, 127–28, 130
Pentecostalism and Charismatic Movements, 127
Pentecostalism and Charismatic Movements in Nigeria, 112, 144
Pentecostalization, 127–28, 131, 135
full-blown, 127
Pentecostalization attest, 130
Pentecostalization of Adventism, 127, 129–30
Pentecostal outpouring, 39
Pentecostal practices, 128, 135
Pentecostal praxis, 128
adaptation of, 127, 130
Pentecostal religious market, 129
Pentecostals, 20, 28, 95, 118, 128
Pentecostal services, 116
Pentecostal train, 117
Pentecostal worldview, 121
People Live, 75
percussion, 110, 128
Performative, 20
Period, x–xi, 8, 10–11, 21, 31, 52, 72, 76–77, 82, 96–97, 100
colonial, 14, 72, 79
shut-door, 8
Pew Research Center, 28, 141

Pew-Templeton Global Religious Futures Project, 145
Phases, 7–9, 14, 30, 35, 37, 42, 45, 68, 72–73
first, 45, 72–73
Pieter Gerard Damsteegt, 10
Pioneers, 27, 29, 42, 67
Pioneer work, 29–30
Pioneer worker, 34
Plateau, 65
Plateau Province, 56–58, 62–63
resident of, 57–59
Plateau resident, 59, 65
platform, 116
Playfair, 65–66
Pluralism, 13, 146
religious, 11
Plurality, 20, 82
Policies, 49, 52, 54, 56, 59, 68, 84–85, 113
policy application, 131
political dimensions, 19
political discipline, 19
political factors, 14
political freedom, 97
Political Organizations, 99–100, 147
political shifts, 4
political turmoil, 131
politics, 47, 58, 75, 99–100, 127, 139
Politics and Identity Formation in Southeastern Nigeria, 139
polygamists, 82, 84, 124
Polygamous marriages, 82, 86
Polygamy, 16, 69, 71, 81–82, 84–86, 93, 95, 131, 140, 145–46
Polygamy and Marriage Relationship, 82, 139
Popoola, T. K., 101
local, 61
Port Harcourt, 129
Portuguese Catholic missionaries, 47
Portuguese ships, 71
position, 50, 57, 64, 69, 71, 75, 85–86, 95

INDEX

possession, 125
Post, Ken, 72, 145
postcolonial, 10, 14
    parallel development of, 17, 26
potential, 22–23, 127, 132, 135
poverty, 19, 105
power, 39, 52, 60, 86–90, 99, 103–4, 125–27
    colonial, 51
    healing, 89
    political, 79
    social, 79
power politics, 52, 137
power relations, 70, 86
practices, 1, 70–71, 76–78, 82, 84–85, 92–93, 108, 111, 114–17, 120, 124, 130, 135
    cultural, 69, 77–78, 92, 122
    heathenish, 76
    polygamous, 85
    private dentistry, 31
practitioners, 33, 52, 82
Praise God, 5
praxis, 91, 134
    denominational, 133
    ecclesial, 92
Pray, 88, 99, 108–9
Prayer Book, 53
Prayers, 87–89, 105, 110, 115, 129, 146
Preaching, 8, 56, 70, 91, 123
    itinerant, 31
pre-marriage preparations, 77
Premillennialism, 142
    pessimist, 81, 100
Preparing Converts, 100
Present Truth, 34, 134, 146
Present Truth and Signs of the Times, 143
preservation, 55, 117, 130, 135
president, 35, 57, 84, 101, 107
    foreign, 113
    indigenous, 113
    local conference, 111

Problem of Colonialism, 70
process, xi, 49, 78–79, 88, 97, 118, 125–26, 131–34
    iterative, 8
Progress in Northern Nigeria, 42, 142
prosperity preaching, 129
Protestant missionaries, 29, 48, 53
Protestant missions, 54, 74
Protestants, 8–9, 28, 71
Protestant theology, 9
Protestant tradition, 10
protests, 79, 100–101
    anti-tax, 78
providential, ix, 23
province, 55, 66
Public Life Global Christianity, 28, 145
publishing houses, 13
pushing, 66

Quarterly Review of the European Division of Seventh-day Adventists, 142

RCM (Roman Catholic Mission), 56
Red Cross, 105
Regions, 13–14, 29, 33, 35, 39, 42–43, 49, 56, 73, 79, 101, 107, 123
    northern, 36, 48–49, 61
    western, 36
Religion, 28, 47–48, 50, 128, 130–31, 139, 145
    foreign, 122
    traditional, 33, 52, 124, 137
Religion in Calabar, 124, 141
reorganization, 63, 102
Revelation, 9, 71
reverberations, 110, 113
reverse mission, 16
Review, 3, 90, 138, 141, 144–45
Revival activities, 114
Revival experience, 113

INDEX

Revivals, 24, 26, 108–12, 115, 117, 125, 127–28, 130
   historic, 113, 128
   religious, 104, 115
Reynaud, Daniel, 9, 145
Rites, 70, 76–78
   fattening, 78
Rituals, 18, 108
rivalry, 44, 47, 57, 61, 65
   bitter, 66
   unhealthy, 61, 68
Rivers Niger, 57, 61
Roberts, 60–61
Rochester, 140, 146
Rochester Press, 140, 146
rocked, 86, 126
Roman Catholic Mission (RCM), 56
Rosalind Hackett notes, 124
Ross, Kenneth R., 140
Route, 95, 129
Routledge, 143
royal court, 48
Rudolf, P., 35
Rule, colonial, 49, 57
rulers, 36, 53, 99
Rumfan Gwamna, 59, 65

Sabbatarian Adventists, 8
Sabbatarians, 82, 124
   indigenous, 124
Sabbath, 10, 32–33, 36, 81, 108, 117, 121, 129–30
   counterfeit, 100
Sabbath-keepers, 34
   indigenous, 33, 39
Sabbath-keeping groups, 81
   indigenous, 34, 82
Sabbath meetings, 41
Sabbath morning, 71
Sabbath School, 113, 133–34
Sabbath School Lesson Quarterly, 87, 145
The Sabbath Sentinel, 138
Sabbath services, 41, 108–9

Sabbath teachings, 67
Sabbath truth, 81
Sabbath worship, 67
Sabinah, 83
Sacra Theologia, 144
Sampson, 82–83, 85
Samson, Jane, 70, 145
Samuel Ajayi Crowther, 48
San Diego, 144
Sao, 36–37, 122
Satan, 91
Satanic counterfeits, 40, 87
Saturday God and Adventism in Ghana, 30, 32, 145
Scandinavian missionaries, 107
Scandinavians, 110
Schisms, 14, 40, 79, 86, 91, 98, 138
Scholarly works, 68, 70
scholars, 8–11, 18, 34, 61, 95
   key, 7
Scholarship, ix–x, 9, 12
Scholastica Ahiazunwa, 139
Schools, 13, 33, 37, 43, 60, 74, 97–98, 101, 106–7, 121–22
   girls, 76
   informal, 39
   primary, 38
   semiformal, 42, 68
SCM (Student Christian Movement), 112–13
Scripture, 134
Scripture Union, 112
SDA. *See* Seventh-day Adventist
Seventh-day Adventist Historiography, 11, 143
Seventh-day Adventist History, 123, 141
Seventh-day Adventist History in West Africa, 36–37, 137
Seventh-day Adventist mission, 2, 7, 13, 53, 59–60, 64, 65, 143–44, 146
Seventh-day Adventist missionaries, 2, 26, 147

INDEX

Seventh-day adventist mission historiography, 9–27
Seventh-Day Adventist Mission Nigerian Branch, 60, 141
Seventh-day Adventists, 22, 28–29, 33, 60, 63–64, 96, 137, 141, 143, 145–46
Seventh-day Adventists Archives, 140, 143, 145
Seventh-day Adventists in Yorubaland, 27, 29, 137
Seventh-day Adventist Yearbook, 30–31, 35, 145
Seventh-day Church, 40, 90
Shankar, 59, 145
Shao, 37, 122
Shape and Flow, 17–20
Shaw, J. L., 31, 143, 145
Sherman A. Nagel Jr., 105
Shift, x, 8–12, 15–18, 112
  critical, 8
  deliberate, 3, 20
  historiographical, 11, 27
  paradigm, 9, 12
Shinmyo, 14, 146
Shobana, 145
Shobana Shankar, 58
shut-door, 8
shut-door theory, 8
sick people, 67
Siebenten-Tags-Adventisten im Nationalsozialismus, 13, 141
Sierra, 31
Sierra Leone, x, 30, 35–36, 38, 40, 42–43, 45, 68, 73
Sierra Lone, 36
Sievert Gustavsson, 107
Silver Spring, xi, 82, 137, 141, 143–45
S.I.M., 62, 64, 66
SIM. *See* Sudan Inland Mission
SIM missionaries, 67
SIM of Kagoro, 60
Simon, 42, 67
singing hymns, 110

Sir Hasketh Bell, 52
Sir Hugh Clifford, 54, 72
Sister Hyde, 41
site, 54, 56, 58–66
skills, entrepreneurial, 37, 122
Slavic cultures, 13
Smith, Uriah, 9
Society, xi, 69–71, 75, 78, 80, 83, 85–86, 95, 100, 112, 118, 129, 135
  conglomerate, 72
  non-Muslim, 50, 61
Sokoto, 53
Sokoto Caliphate, 50
Solademi, Pastor G., 113–14
Søren Kierkegaard, 5
Sosoki village, 46
south, 34, 45, 48–51, 63, 73, 107, 116, 121
South America, 12–14
Southeast, 38–40, 46, 80, 97, 101, 104–5, 107, 118, 123
Southeast Mission, 39
Southeast Nigeria, 34, 39, 96, 138–39
Southeast of Nigeria, 29, 38, 43, 86, 94, 121, 123
Southeast regions, 40, 79, 86
Southern, 44, 48–49
Southern Borno Province, 56
Southern Nigeria, 26, 28, 32–33, 45, 71, 138
Southern Provinces, 58
Southern Zaria, 56, 59
South Korea, 115
South Nigeria, 39, 139
Southwest, 48
South-Western Nigeria, 138
Southwestern Nigerian Mission, 45
SPCK, 142
spearheaded, 97, 118, 128–29
Special Reference, 146
Spectrum, 3, 120, 142
Spectrum Magazine, 2

speech, 99–100
Spes Christiana, 2–3, 94, 147
Spheres of influence, xi, 44, 47, 56–58, 61, 63–66, 68
Spheres of Influence of Missionary Societies, 57, 139
Spicer, William A., 9
Spiritism, 86, 125
spirit movement, 39, 87, 89, 91
Spirits, 25, 40, 87, 90, 116, 125
spirituality, 17, 109–10, 116
  grassroots, 19
springboard, 34
springboard plan, 9
springing, 90, 127
stages, 1–2, 11, 26
starvation, 105–6
Starve, 147
stations, 32, 39, 41, 58–59, 62–63
Statistics, 102, 137
status quo, 55, 127, 129
Stock, 3
stockfish, 105
stories, ix, 3, 18, 20–21, 61, 68, 83, 86, 104, 106, 139
Stratification, 146
Structure and Conflict, 72
Structure and Conflict in Nigeria, 145
Student Christian Movement (SCM), 112–13
student groups, 128
student leaders, 128
student movements, 127
students, 33, 38–39, 81, 98, 108–15, 122–23, 127–28
  fellow, 33, 113
  non-Adventist, 128
style, camp-meeting-booth, 123
subaltern spiritualities, 24
subculture, 92, 104
  substitute, 78
Sudan, 51
Sudan Inland Mission (SIM), 47, 52, 56–57, 61–68

Sudan Interior Mission, 63, 140
Superintendent, 41, 46, 57, 99, 123
Sydney, 32–34

Tanzanian culture, 70
Tatuí, 141
taxes, 79, 99
teachers, 4, 33–34, 37, 76, 101, 134
Teachers' Training Institute, 33
Teacher's Training School, 74, 97
theological thinking, 132–33, 135
  constructive, 133
theology, 2, 9, 22, 91, 120, 133–35, 141
shut-door, 7
Thompson, W. A., 53
Thompstone, E. W., 65, 146
Thomson, Graeme, 54–56
threats, 50–51, 103
Three-Self Patriotic Movement, 14
Tikili, 33–34, 38, 40, 43, 45, 73, 81, 87–90
  Benjamin I., x, 29–30, 32–33, 42, 45, 73, 146
  contribution of, 39, 87
  resignation of, 40, 90
  unfortunate disassociation of, 39, 87
Toleration, 53, 77, 84
tongues, 40, 87, 110, 113, 125
Toronto Industrial Mission, 51
Towers, Charles L., 52
Traditions, 1, 20, 29, 72, 78, 85, 113, 119, 121–22, 124, 143
  denominational, 131
  ecclesial, 91
  ethnic, 4
  evangelical, 9
  historiographical, 17, 26
  missionary-transferred, 130
Trailblazers, 72–73, 123
Trailblazers of Adventism in Nigeria, 2, 29, 45, 147
transcend past difficulties, 23

INDEX

transfer, 83
transformation, 20, 104, 135
Transforming Mission, 24, 70, 138
transition, 9
translation, 14, 53, 77, 134
   contextual, 134
transplantation, 4, 134
treatment, 41, 67, 78, 82, 92–93
   historical, 43
   medical, 41, 67
tree standing, 88
Trenton, 142, 144
Trevor, 145
Trials, 138
Trials and Victories, 36
tribalism, 131
tribe, 62–63, 71, 134
Trim, David J. B., 2, 11, 102, 146
Trim, D. J. B., ix, xi, 11–13, 102
triumphalist, 9, 19
triumphalist attitude, 92
Turaki, 50, 97
Turner, W. G., 105, 146
Twentieth century, 9, 29, 48, 138

Ubah, C. N., 54–56, 146
Ukegbu, J. O., 108, 146
Umueze, 105
United States, 2, 31, 45, 73, 117, 129, 133–34
University, 2, 108–10, 112–13, 138–40, 142, 144–46
The Unknown Secrets of Prosperity, 129, 137

Van Allen, 75, 146
Van Gelder, 117, 130, 146
Vickers, Michael, 72, 145
Victory Sanctuary Seventh-day Adventist Church, 137
Vine, Mary J., 71, 76–77, 83, 85–86, 146
Violence in Nigeria, 103, 140

Visions, ix, 5, 8, 11, 40, 43, 69, 87–90, 92, 125–26, 140, 145
   anticipatory, 3, 17, 20
   disillusioned, 112
   eschatological, 93
   just missionary, 27

Waggoner, Ellet J., 8
Walls, Andrew F., 18, 37, 146
War, 79, 94–96, 104–6, 118
   political ethnic, 105
   religious, 105
Warrant chiefs, 79
   ordered local, 79
Warri, 71
wartime, 118
Washington, 138, 140, 145
Washington D.C., 60
Watford, 67, 142
Watson, Noelle, 48, 146
The Way People Live, 144
West, 34, 38, 40, 45–46, 48–49, 73, 85, 97–98, 107, 116, 128
West Africa, 30–32, 35, 39, 42, 46, 80, 82, 97, 99, 139, 141–43
West African, 26, 30, 34–36, 45, 73, 101
West African Advent Messenger, 99, 138–39, 142, 147
West African Christianity, 20, 145
West African mission, 35, 57
West African Union, 101
West African Union Mission, 107
West African Union of SDA Church, 101, 143
West Coast of Africa, 41, 139
Western, 28
Western Adventism, 94, 102, 124
Western Nigeria, 27, 29, 36, 45, 70, 101, 108, 111, 142, 144
White, 5, 9, 97–98, 146
   Ellen G., 5, 9, 14, 109, 131, 146
Widening Horizons, 71, 82, 143

INDEX

Wife, 30–32, 35, 37–38, 41, 67, 83–85
William, Timothy Jones, 30–31, 83, 85–86, 146
William's heart, 83
Wilson, 105–6
   Neal C., 147
Wogu, Chigemezi N., ix–xi, 9, 12–13, 44–45, 72–73, 100, 123, 141, 144, 147
Women, 69, 71, 75–81, 83, 85–86, 89, 92, 95, 146
   indigenous, 78, 80–81
   native, 80
   unconverted, 86
   young, 76–77
Women's Institutions in Igbo Society, 75, 140
Women's Riot, 78
Women's War, 79
Women uprising, 80
Workers, 37, 45, 47, 73, 88, 99–101, 123
   fellow, 99
   fellow Christian, 118
   local, 100, 110
   national, 37
   native, 99
World's Christian Population, 145
worldview, 22, 89
   neo-Pentecostal, 129
World War II, xi
Worship, 33, 40, 69, 71, 88, 91, 95, 106, 109–11, 116–18, 128–29, 134
   ancestor, 70, 125
   vibrant, 90
Worship atmosphere, 128
Worship days, 105

Worship ethos, 130
Worship praxis, 128
Worship rituals, 132
Worship services, 110, 130
Worship spaces, 128
Worship style, 91, 110
   vibrant, 110, 128
Wosu, Robert O., 99–100, 147

Yaba Church, 116
Yearbook, 45
Yearbook of Seventh-day Adventists, 31
Yoruba Adventists, 111
Yoruba conversions, 122
Yorubaland, 36, 48
Yoruba language, 36
   local, 36
Yorubas, 36, 46, 122–24
Young men, 76, 83, 85, 104
Young people, 108, 111, 113, 116, 128, 134–35
The Youth Instructor, 142
Youths, 101, 111–12, 114, 116, 131
Youth's Instructor, 142
Yowere, 46
Yusufu Turaki, 140

Zagon Katab, 66
Zagon Kataf, 64–65
Zangon Katab, 62–63
Zangon Kataf, 59–62, 64–67
Zaria, 47, 60–63, 65, 139, 142–43
   resident of, 60, 62, 64–66
Zaria City, 51, 54
Zaria Division, 61
Zaria Province, 60, 65–66, 144, 146
Zeitgeist, 57, 77
Zongon Katab, 62–63

www.ingramcontent.com/pod-product-compliance
Lightning Source LLC
Chambersburg PA
CBHW062045220426
43662CB00010B/1656